Content Matters

Social Studies in the Elementary and Middle School

Leif Fearn and Eric Fearn

Rowman & Littlefield Education
A division of
ROWMAN & LITTLEFIELD PUBLISHERS, INC.
Lanham • New York • Toronto • Plymouth, UK

Published by Rowman & Littlefield Education
A division of Rowman & Littlefield Publishers, Inc.
A wholly owned subsidary of The Rowman & Littlefield Publishing Group, Inc.
4501 Forbes Boulevard, Suite 200, Lanham, Maryland 20706
www.rowman.com

10 Thornbury Road, Plymouth PL6 7PP, United Kingdom

British Library Cataloguing in Publication Information Available

Library of Congress Cataloging-in-Publication Data

Fearn, Leif.
  Content matters : social studies in the elementary and middle school / Leif Fearn and
Eric Fearn.
     pages ; cm
  Includes bibliographical references.
  ISBN 978-1-61048-950-8 (cloth : alk. paper) — ISBN 978-1-61048-951-5 (pbk. : alk.
paper) — ISBN 978-1-61048-952-2 (ebook) 1. Social sciences—Study and teaching
(Elementary)—United States. 2. Social sciences—Study and teaching (Middle school)—
United States. 3. Social sciences—Study and teaching—Standards—United States.
I. Title.
  LB1584.F43 2013
  300.71—dc23
                                                                                       2013009873

Printed in the United States of America

From Leif:
to The Writing Haven Writers,
warriors all, who know the difference
between making arguments and having arguments.

From Eric: to my family.

Contents

Acknowledgments

We acknowledge the contributions of many people in this adventure into the content of the social studies. We thank Houston Burnside, Sue Reynolds, Jeanne Stone, Nancy Farnan, Jeanne Jenkins, and Paul McHenry for their reading and critique of early manuscripts. We specifically thank Arnold Fenton for his counsel regarding the distinction between economics and personal finance and Nancy Farnan for her inestimable skill and care in preparation of the manuscript.

We recognize Betty Abel Jurus, for this book would not exist had she not given forty minutes one morning years ago to teach Leif every writer's essentials. We thank Ron D. Allen, Assiniboine Cree, great friend, who looked Leif in the eye one cold February morning and said I must never forget who I came to know from the tribes and what I learned from them and theirs.

Eric is indebted to professors Davis, Vanderwood, and Head at San Diego State University for their profound influence on his professional and cultural education.

And we thank our teachers who left us knowing there is much to learn, and we'll just have to figure it out. That is, to a large extent, pretty much why we are both essentially self-taught. We hope we have left our students knowing there is much to learn, they'll just have to figure it out, and to a large extent, they will live self-taught lives.

Introduction

This book is about *what* we teach in the social studies, not how. The primary audience is teacher candidates in professional education programs. Secondarily, the audience is both novice and experienced teachers in professional development. The book is not about how to teach geography or personal finance; it is about what we teach when we teach geography and personal finance. The distinction is important.

Just as all social studies curricula and textbooks rest upon selections, this book reflects our selections and definitions of social studies content. We have selected history, geography, personal finance, native peoples, the Constitution, the Declaration of Independence, world religions, biographical studies, current events, and the literacy (writing) necessary to teach and learn in the social studies. Each of the ten chapters is titled with one of the content areas and defines what that content area means for instruction.

Readers must understand that there are more social studies to teach than there is time to teach social studies. There is more history, personal finance, world religions, and native peoples to read and write about than there is page space on which to publish a text. There are always more social studies to teach, so writers and teachers have to make selections. This book reflects ours.

Textbook writers accumulate what they know, calculate dictated page space restraints, and select *in* what is most crucial, which means much of merit is not selected *in*.

Social studies students should learn how writers and teachers select what appears in the social studies books and courses of study. Perhaps we need social studies lessons or whole units about how writers, publishers, and teachers select what to write, publish, and teach.

Think of the study that constitutes the anchor in the social studies—history. Social studies could as easily be anchored in biographical studies or current events.

But the anchor is characteristically history. The selection question is *what to teach when we are teaching history*. It is a content question, not a procedure question.

If our selections are not accurate, but we have accurate procedural knowledge, it is possible that when we think we are teaching history, we are, in fact, teaching the wrong stuff, or not much at all, but brilliantly? It wouldn't be the first time. Many perfectly brilliant teachers have taught students to name sentence parts when they thought they were teaching writing. It is not that knowing the names of sentence parts is wrong; it is that the ability to name sentence parts, for most people, is unrelated to the ability to write a sentence.

Translated to history, it isn't that dates and apparent facts are not good to know; it is that dates and apparent facts are not necessarily related to being historically literate. Students often report that they have been bored with history in their K–12 schooling. When asked what their history classes were like, many say they had to memorize facts, dates, wars, and people's names. They weren't bored by history; they were bored by history instruction.

What does it mean to be *historically literate*? We will use the term *literate* often in this book. Being *literate* in history means being able to think in relationships between then and now, which means comparing and contrasting.

Historically literate people think in questions, and they need material with which to think. In history, the material is information, data, apparent facts, and lines of evidence. Historical literacy is thinking and the material with which to think.

Thinking in history isn't boring. It can be almost thrilling if instruction capitalizes on the prior knowledge students bring to history class. What they know best is story grammar, and every historical instance they are ever expected to learn has characters, settings, problems, resolutions, and consequences, both intended and unintended. The gold rush might be more compelling if it included Levi Strauss and Jack London, the perfectly rotten geographic conditions in both California and Alaska, the fact that almost no one got much of anything out of it, but it put both California and Alaska on the map.

The apparent historical evidence is like rings in a tree trunk. At first glance they tell how many, but within the rings are biological and anthropological inferences (Collingwood 1965, xiv, xv). It is the construction of inferences that is interesting. The rings are just rings. The evidence, such as it is, is just testimony. Properly conceived, history instruction helps students read the rings and find relationships between and among the rings. To merely count the rings might seem boring, but to understand the rings is very different.

Think about personal finance as content in the social studies. This is the social study that receives, possibly, the least of the social studies attention, while it is probably the most crucial study as any in the comprehensive curriculum. In a relatively free enterprise economy, some people have less than enough, some have about enough, and some more than enough. The curricular question is how to be one of the people with enough, or more than enough, but not less than enough.

Students can *begin* to engage in such "an economic way of thinking" (Miller and VanFossen 2008, 287–88) when they are nine or ten years old.

Students can begin growing geographically literate when they are five or six years old. It isn't merely the location of Cleveland, though their mental maps that show Cleveland are part of geographic literacy. What students need to learn is that geography matters. *Why Geography Matters* (de Blij 2005) suggests three reasons why geography matters: global terrorism, the rise of China, and global climate change. While memorizing the capitals of every state is an impressive feat, it doesn't matter very much, and it has little to do with being geographically literate.

What does matter for geographic literacy is knowing what migration meant many hundreds of thousands of years ago and what it continues to mean today. Geography explains part of Alexander's rise to becoming "great," what happened when Napoleon marched into a Russian winter, why armies fail when they march into someone else's territory and do not have someone else's cooperation, and what Lake Baikal means to the world. Geographic literacy means understanding relationships between geography and other social studies.

The study of native peoples adds texture to the social studies. Students usually learn something about native peoples who live nearby or in their state, and it is useful for students in southwest Ohio to know about Shawnee. But there are also Walpi, Oriabi, and Moenkopi, Hopi villages in northeast Arizona, and four Apache peoples in New Mexico and Arizona. Pimas live in Arizona, Quileute and Makah in Washington, and Cherokee in North Carolina and Oklahoma.

And what does it mean to study our nation's founding documents? Most students probably memorize the preamble to the United States Constitution, and most likely take tests on the Constitution and the Declaration of Independence. But when those students think the president runs the country and can raise and lower taxes, it is clear that they studied the wrong content.

Nothing in the social studies is more important than "who." We do not have to engage in hero worship to recognize that nothing happens by itself, that whatever happens (not including tectonic shifts and hurricanes) is due to what people think, feel, and do.

Social studies students must come to know who the people are and understand why they are worthy of study. The second part of that sentence is very important. Even children in kindergarten know Benjamin Franklin. Kindergarten teachers fold him into February units on presidents Washington and Lincoln. Why learn about Franklin? Children and youth need to learn why he is worthy of their attention.

What makes a person sufficiently remarkable to merit study? What are the criteria? Why study Thomas Edison and Dolores Huerta? Why do we know so much about Thomas Jefferson and so little about John Adams? Who was the founder of Ragtime, of Tin Pan Alley, of the minstrel, of the book musical? Who were the people who wrote the songs in *The Great American Songbook*?

Some people say that our species' primary cultural marker is religion. World religions, as social studies content, can begin with biographical studies. Who was Abraham? Among the most prominent world religions three are called "Abrahamic" because all three count Abraham as their first and primary prophet. He is as legitimate a biographical study as William the Conqueror, Genghis Khan, Leonardo da Vinci, or Joan of Arc. Biographical study in world religions is no more or less a part of the social studies than is history and geography.

Finally, and woven through all of the social studies content areas introduced earlier, is what most people refer to as "current events." In fact, the study is how to listen to, watch, and read the media for the purpose of being informed. What students come to know from print and electronic media is how social studies content informs what they read, see, and hear in the media every day.

That is how we conceptualize social studies content in this book. A map metaphor reveals how the content plays out in the hands of social studies teachers. Suppose we plan a road trip from Waco, Texas, to Shippensburg, Pennsylvania. Our map shows many routes between Waco and Shippensburg. But essentially, we head northeast from Waco. We can see Arkansas, if we like, or miss it altogether. If we have friends in Leavenworth, Kansas, or Cedar Falls, Iowa, we can stop along the way and still head northeast.

The road map is not a directive for driving from Waco to Shippensburg, and this book is not a directive for teaching and learning about social studies. The book is a guide, a frame. Readers should use its definitions and examples to construct units of study that take their elementary and middle school students on interesting journeys into and through the social studies content areas.

Linda Salvucci, chair of the National Council for History Education, said that "History is very much being shortchanged" (Dillon 2011). It is not substantively different with geography, partly because much of the geography we teach still does not fulfill the promise of modern conceptions of geography *content*.

The argument here is not that social studies *content* was better taught and learned in some golden "good old days" before the advent of integrated units of study in the social studies. Social studies content was never taught very well. There never was a time when Americans knew much history and geography, or constitutional structures and applications, or even how to read a newspaper critically.

The point in this book is that we are missing the opportunity that integrated social studies offers, precisely because we think more about *how* to teach social studies units than about *what* we teach when we teach social studies units. The point is not whether we should arrange the social studies in units of study. Among the variety of investigations of integrated social studies unit instruction (Levstik and Tyson 2008, 54–55), there are no direct efficacy data, as in, "If we do these kinds of things with these kinds of students for this range of time, we increase the probability of getting this kind of performance in history, geography, and Constitutional knowledge." But the absence of evidence is not evidence of absence. Unit organization depends on *what is in units of study*, not whether they exist.

Not only do we focus more on procedures than on content; we do not even give the social studies the time of day. The commitment of time is positively related to performance on U.S. history tests (NAEP 2007). Ask students what is important in the curriculum, and compare their answers with what "subjects" get the most time. It is not hard to understand why so many students perform below reasonable expectations on tests of history knowledge and inferential thinking in history.

In this book we focus on content instruction *as described* in these content chapters. The study of personal finance, for example, is described as how to acquire and manage resources. We need to teach students how to be effective *participants* in a relatively free enterprise economy, how to be part of the minority of people who know how to use and benefit from the economy. Personal finance is about understanding the accumulation and management of resources.

Every teacher has strengths, interests, passions, and experiences that are relevant to the social studies. What if the second grade teacher or the fourth or the seventh grade teacher grew up within sight of the Sawtooth Mountains in Idaho or at the foot of Iron Mountain in Alabama? Those teachers might emphasize Joseph of the Nez Perce or Vulcan, Roman god of fire.

We teach to what is expected of us, of course, and left to our own devices, we teach to our strengths, our passions, our backgrounds. We teach best what interests us. A third grade teacher who was a competitive athlete in high school and college includes biographical studies, history, geography, and rule books in the sports world. A teacher enthralled by Carl Sandburg uses "Who Was That Early Sodbuster" to texture studies of westward exploration.

What about a teacher whose hobby is gray wolves? There are no gray wolf standards. This is a teacher who understands how social studies content can be, should be, integrated throughout the comprehensive curriculum.

We'll name this teacher Van. We'll say she teaches in Cheswold, Delaware, and fourth grade teachers in her district teach about the Gold Rush. She opens a book one Tuesday afternoon immediately after lunch and begins to read aloud: "Buck did not read the newspapers, or he would have known that trouble was brewing, not alone for himself, but for every tidewater dog, strong of muscle and with warm, long hair, from Puget Sound to San Diego" (London 1994, 445).

She stops and waits a second or two. "Listen again, boys and girls. What do you notice?"

Gregor says he thinks it's about a dog. Renie says it's a really big and strong dog. Janice asks what tidewater means, and Sofia asks where Puget Sound is. Van writes on the board: Puget Sound, San Diego, tidewater, strong of muscle, trouble is brewing, Dover.

So far, there is locational geography, history, idiomatic language, and what "tidewater" means. That is on the first day, the first sentence. By Tuesday of the following week, they are in California and looking north.

Soon they are in the Yukon Territory, and some dogs have a peculiar look about them. Their feet are bigger, their chests deeper, and their shoulders more heavily muscled than the rest of their bodies, their tails curl up and over their backs, and at night, some of them lie quietly while others yip and bark, until a wail rises over the nearest forested ridge, and those peculiar-looking dogs sit on their rumps and answer back, and when they're all howling at once, the harmonies make human neck hair stand at attention. Van is where she needs to be to make her hobby part of her curriculum.

What of the Gold Rush? That is where those dogs are. That is where Jack London's story is set. Integrated social studies instruction isn't just about the Gold Rush; it is about the big picture, the prime concept, the fabric. Fourth grade Gold Rush isn't Sutter's Mill. It is the Atlantic and Pacific Oceans, the coast of South America, horses and oxen in what became Kansas and Colorado, wealth for the precious few who found enough gold to matter, Chinese immigration, railroads, Yukon Territory, Alaska, snow and cold, native peoples, and dogs. Van's Gold Rush unit is all of that, if she pleases, but she emphasizes the dogs and their ancestors.

Remember that Van teaches history, geography, money, biography, native peoples, transportation, communication, communities, and regions. And she is reading from Newbery Medal literature by an iconic American writer. She is posing reader response questions that emphasize interactions between reader and text (Rosenblatt 1978). She teaches basic wolf biology and the relationship between wolf as a social predator and the North's ungulate (hoofed) population.

She teaches ratio because wolves eat a fourth of their body weight on a fresh kill. She teaches how literature affects people's ideas and ideals because both oral and written literature are primarily responsible for making the wolf an endangered species.

Does all of that seem terribly complex for a class of nine-year-olds? It won't by the end of their fourth grade year with Van. What if the children don't care as much about wolves as Van does? They will because she does. Children and adults tend to care about what they come to know, children tend to care about what their teachers care about, and they come to know as they construct their fabric. That is what instructional integration through the social studies means and does.

The social studies are fused because the social studies require fusion. Van *uses* the literature; she doesn't merely put it in. She *uses* the mathematics to give meaning to the science embedded in her social studies.

There might be a third, or a seventh, grade teacher, who marvels at the mathematical purity of Mozart's piano Concertos 20 and 21. What are your passions, your interests? Were you born in Hawaii? Do you ski Alta or Stowe? Do you read poetry? Raise Dobermans? Were you ever on a cheer squad? Do you dance, play fantasy football, or grow vegetables in your yard? How do you use the social studies to teach Homer in a sixth grade? Or Vietnam in a fifth grade? Or Poland in a fourth? Those aren't in the sixth, fifth, or fourth grade books and standards? Of course they are. We teach history, not someone's history; rather, history as a way of knowing and thinking.

We teach literature in the social studies because reading is to unzip a book, step inside, zip it up again, and meander about awhile so when we leave, there are pieces of the book stuck to us forever. Some of the pieces are historic, some geographic, some biographical, and some artistic. When we read Gary Paulsen's *The Winter Room* (1989) we find that literature is humorous and pathetic (in the sense of pathos), at once, and we get to teach what "pathos" means and help young people look for it in good literature we select to give special texture to the social studies.

Our standards are part of the fabric, as well. Every social studies standard is an integrated curricular day or week or month just waiting for an interesting and interested teacher who understands content sufficiently well to breathe life into it. The standards are waiting for the teacher. The students are waiting for the teacher. Social studies teachers who understand integrated curriculum as the weaving of content must not fail the standards or the students.

REFERENCES

Collingwood, Robin. 1965. *Essays in the Philosophy of History.* Austin: University of Texas Press.

De Blij, Harm. 2005. *Why Geography Matters: Three Challenges Facing America.* New York: Oxford University Press.

Dillon, Sam. 2011. *The New York Times: Education.* www.nytimes.com/2011/06/15/education/15history.html.

Levstik, Linda S., and Cynthia A. Tyson. 2008. *Handbook of Research in Social Studies Education.* New York: Routledge.

London, Jack. 1994. *Call of the Wild.* In *Jack London: Tales of the North*, 445–447. Secaucus, NJ: Castle.

Miller, Steven L., and Phillip J. VanFossen. 2008. "Recent Research on the Teaching and Learning of Pre-collegiate Economics." In *Handbook of Research in Social Studies Education*, edited by Linda S. Levstik and Cynthia A. Tyson, 284–304. New York: Routledge.

NAEP (National Assessment of Educational Progress). 2007. 2006 U.S. History. Retrieved July 12, 2007, from http://ncea.ed.gov/nationsreportcard/ushistory/.

Paulsen, Gary. 1989. *The Winter Room*. New York: Bantam Doubleday Dell.

Rosenblatt, Louise M. 1978. *The Reader, The Text, The Poem: The Transactional Theory of the Literary Work*. Carbondale: Southern Illinois University Press.

CHAPTER 1

Biographical Studies

People of Note

Think about it. In the social studies, what isn't biography? What is there that is not about what people have done or what people are doing, or the influence of people on what lies ahead? You could wrap the entire social studies program around biographical studies. Science, too, and the aesthetics, literature, and physical education. Much of a student's education could be about who the people are and the reasons why we need to know them.

If Ralph Waldo Emerson's observation is true, that "There is properly no history; only biography," then knowledge of history is biographical, or narratives made by characters. Perhaps we sometimes forget Euclid when we teach geometry, Michelangelo when we teach art, and Isaac Newton when we teach science. This chapter is about not forgetting, precisely because we make biographical studies a fundamental area of social studies content.

THE CONTENT FOR TEACHING BIOGRAPHICAL STUDIES

Let us begin in Kansas. Kansas is in the middle of the continental United States. Ellsworth used to be the middle city (central Kansas) in the United States, but now the central city in the United States is Lebanon (north central Kansas).

Kansas social studies standards (1999, 18) in grades two, four, and six name sixty-four biographical studies. Several appear more than once through the three grades. The list of sixty-four begins in the second grade.

Why not teach Michelangelo (Kansas sixth grade) in the fourth grade, Marco Polo (Kansas second grade) in the sixth, and Clara Barton (Kansas fourth grade) in the second or the sixth? And Alf Landon? Carrie Nation? Gordon Parks? Clyde Cessna? Who are they, and why do they appear on the Kansas fourth grade list?

Remember, Alf Landon, Carrie Nation, Gordon Parks, and Clyde Cessna were either born or worked or they died in Kansas. But if you live in New Jersey, do you have to know Carrie Nation? Perhaps not, unless you want to understand early twentieth-century constitutional history. Alf Landon ran against Franklin Roosevelt in 1936. Gordon Parks was an eminent photographer, and Clyde Cessna made his mark in aviation.

It isn't hero worship (Hook 1992). It is recognition that, as Isaac Newton remarks, "If I have seen farther, it is by standing on the shoulders of giants." For Newton, the giants were Kepler, Brahe, Copernicus, and Galileo, to name several. They aren't necessarily heroes, certainly not in the sense of being heroic in today's constitutional republic, where heroism is defined as "any individual who does his work well and makes a unique contribution to the public good" (Hook 1992, 153). Rather, they are people who set the stage, even as Newton set the stage for Max Planck, Albert Einstein, Neils Bohr, Leo Sizlard, and Robert Rutherford, who followed.

Tallied up in the earlier paragraph, there are nine sets of shoulders. Those belong to people who gave us theories of gravity, laws of motion, knowledge about planetary movement, heliocentricity, improvements on the telescope, theories of tides, the Scientific Revolution, and the Atomic Age. Imagine the science and history our students could learn if they studied those nine and how they changed the world. Think of the science and history they cannot understand if they do not know those people.

Consider the range of social studies students could learn if they studied those nine. Think of the history, the geography, and the economics. Think of the history of world religions that opens when students study Galileo. We'd have to include at least four popes and a dozen additional people of note (including Aristotle from nearly 2,000 years before). We would study the Inquisition and what that meant in historical perspective. The fabric would demand attention to European geography and the geography of the solar system. We would run out of year well before we ran out of biographies, history, geography, government, and world religions if we decided to study only Galileo.

Biographical studies is knowing people who have made a difference and the difference they made. Edvard Grieg made a difference, as did Beethoven, Tchaikovsky, Rachmaninov, Haydn, Mozart, Schubert, Vivaldi, and Handel, not for mere "music appreciation," but as the distinction between music and noise, and an appreciation for the species that produced such extraordinary talents. After all, those musical giants are members of the species homo erectus who left Africa and Asia 1.8 million years ago and populated the world (Collins 2006, 126; King 2002, 93).

In 1948, 1949, 1950, and 1952, Bob Mathias ruled the world of track and field as a decathlete; in 1953 and 1956, it was Milt Campbell; and in 1956, 1958, and 1960, Rafer Johnson. Along the way there were C. K. Yang (1959) and Vasily Kuznetso (1958, 1962). Those were the greatest athletes in the world between 1948 and 1964. They are heroic, if heroes are the ones who live their lives well and make a difference.

Why devote a paragraph to decathletes in a social studies chapter on biographies? They are people of note. We can use them in studies of geography and history, at least. What, for example, is noteworthy about 1948 (London), 1956 (Melbourne), or 1960 (Rome)? Where is Vasily Kuznetsov's Soviet Union on a world map? Why can we find it on a map published in 1948, 1956, and 1960, but not on a map published in 2000?

What happened to those men? One of them was a U.S. Congressman. One of them knelt beside the wounded Robert Kennedy on the floor where he fell when he was shot by Sirhan Sirhan in a Los Angeles hotel kitchen. What could we do with all that in a social studies lesson segment, or even a portion of a unit?

Almost no one knows who Milt Campbell and Rafer Johnson are, "relates" to them, remembers them, or cares much about them. In fact, among our first graders, almost no one knows George Washington, Abraham Lincoln, Martin Luther King Jr., or Sojourner Truth. Almost no six-year-old "relates" to people who lived two hundred years ago, or twenty years ago, for that matter.

While few if any kindergartners know or care about Washington and Lincoln, we teach them anyway, and then in the first grade and in the second again, and then in third, fourth, and fifth. In time, students come to know them, remember them from the previous year, care about them and, therefore, "relate" to them. Biographical studies is about helping students come to know what makes people worthy of remembering, of caring about, of being noteworthy.

The people we teach do not have to be founders of our country or responsible for a national movement. They can be Isaac Asimov whom many people credit with being the father of the golden age of science fiction or at least the man who wrote the rules for robots, or James K. Polk during whose presidency the land mass of the United States nearly doubled, or W. E. B. Du Bois who founded the National Association for the Advancement of Colored People (NAACP) and was one of the half-dozen brightest intellectual lights of the twentieth century, or the Beatles whose music will be iconic in a hundred years, or, perhaps, Ted Williams, who is thought to be the greatest baseball hitter of all time.

Founders, presidents, composers of music, scientists, athletes, writers—all members of that group of people worthy of note, and as we study such people, we come to understand what makes them worthy. Hart (1978) compiled brief biographies in *The 100: A Ranking of the Most Influential Persons in History*. He presented his criteria for selecting and ranking those one hundred from the most influential to the one-hundredth most influential person of all time.

It is important that Hart presented *his* criteria, not *the* criteria. *His* criteria, in general, include:

- influential, though not necessarily great (Hitler is ranked thirty-sixth)
- persons whose effect has been greatest (John F. Kennedy is among the hundred)
- persons whose lives shaped our lives (we live in a nation shaped by James Madison and Martin Luther King Jr.)

- persons of influence, whether noble or reprehensible (both Gandhi and Stalin are among the hundred) (Hart 1978, 26)

There is a similar collection titled *The Black 100: A Ranking of the Most Influential Black Americans* (Salley 1999) with its own criteria for selection and ranking. Simmons (1996) edited *The Scientific 100*, Knauer (1999) edited *Time 100 Builders and Titans*, and Murray (2005) edited *The Most Influential People of the Last 100 Years*. Along the way are similar kinds of collections, among them *Lives of Musicians* (Krull 1993), *The Signers: The 56 Stories behind the Declaration of Independence* (Fradin 1999), and *The Founders: The 39 Stories behind the United States Constitution* (Fradin 2005).

In those several collections of biographies there are more than four hundred people deemed worthy of biographical study. In addition, there is *Biographical Dictionary of Hispanic Americans* (Meyer 2001) and *American Women: A Library of Congress Guide for the Study of Woman's History and Culture in the United States* (Harvey 2005). Those several collections of biographies could be the instructional core of a K–8 biographical study, in which criteria for worthiness is the central focus. Think of the richness of a student's education were they to know only a small portion of the people on the lists, especially with regard to what makes a person worthy of study.

No biography is harder than another. There are no third or seventh grade biographies. They can all be studied and written as story grammars. Biographical studies include everyone and everything. We could start with Mercator (geography), of course, or John Adams (history and government), Alice Roosevelt (Theodore's daughter), or Farley Mowat (writer). Or, readers of this page could rest awhile and think about whom they think is noteworthy, whom they admire. We can teach anyone we decide to teach because the lesson would highlight what makes people noteworthy. But we have to start.

One problem with starting is resources. There are far more biographies than there are books that many children are able to read. There are some collections of biographies for younger readers (Fradin 2002, 2005; Krull 1992), but where do teachers get young reader biographies of Genghis Khan and Steve Jobs? We start by looking everywhere. Then, if we want to introduce third graders to the people who signed the Declaration of Independence, we find a copy of *Lives of the Signers of the Declaration of Independence* (Lossing 2004), select a signer, and write the biography as a story grammar.

Character: The story is about Elbridge Gerry. Other characters include John Adams, Richard Henry Lee, George Washington, and John Marshall.

Setting: Main setting is Massachusetts where he was born at Marblehead in July 1744. His story also takes place in the Continental Congress and France, as an envoy from the United States.

Problem: Elbridge Gerry is known best for his leadership during the period when the Declaration of Independence was argued, drafted, argued again, and signed and when the Constitution was crafted and adopted, then ratified. Because he was intelligent and had a strong background in private business, his advice was listened to and valued. His main problem was how to return to private life after the Constitution was ratified. He thought it his duty to the country to respond when his public called, so he spent the rest of his life as governor of Massachusetts and vice president of the United States.

Synopsis: Elbridge Gerry is probably the most important person not known in the formation of the United States. We all know Washington and Jefferson, but Elbridge Gerry is of equal importance because people who knew him knew his extraordinary abilities. He was a graduate of Harvard College, successful in business, respected for his work on the formation of the United States, and called upon to serve in state and national office. He passed away in November 1814 at the age of seventy.

It took eighteen minutes to read the biography of Elbridge Gerry in Lossing (2004) and write the story grammar. There is a more extensive biography on the Internet. Type Elbridge Gerry in your browser and make the story grammar as extensive as you like. If we were to write one biographical story grammar per week for two school years, we would have four dozen that elementary grade students can read, in addition to published collections for young readers.

Or, we could enlist our colleagues in biographical story grammar writing, once per month for a school year. If there are fifteen teachers at the school, and each wrote a story grammar each month, there would be more than one hundred biographical story grammars bound in a loose-leaf notebook in the school library, or better, one in each classroom. When fourth grader Monica says she read that story grammar about Mozart last year, we tell her to find Mozart on the Internet, and learn enough to add to the page in the loose-leaf notebook. She would begin her search with the prior knowledge from the teachers' story grammar notebook. But we have to start.

APPLICATIONS IN THE CLASSROOM:
PRIMARY, INTERMEDIATE, AND MIDDLE LEVELS

The following three lesson segments, and all for each social studies content area hereafter, fall into three grade ranges: primary (K–2), intermediate (3–5), and middle level (6–8). Each lesson segment appears in seven parts: objective, common core standards, background, vocabulary, comprehensibility and accessibility, procedures, and review and assessment. Drop down to the first lesson segment for biographical studies to see how the seven lesson parts are arranged on one page. We expect that as readers flesh out the lesson segments and their parts, readers will be able to develop the lesson parts on the basis of the brief cues and, thereby, make the lesson segments their own.

Objective: Given that people are more likely to learn what they do than what they are taught, the objective states what students will do. The objective for the biographical studies lesson segment that follows this explanation states that "Second graders will complete a story grammar for a Founder selected from among resources available in the classroom and the school library."

Common Core Standards: The emphasis in these lesson segments is Common Core Standards for English language arts and literacy in history/social studies, science, and technological subjects (Common Core State Standards Initiative, June 2, 2010).

Background: "Background" means prior knowledge. Students' prior knowledge is either assumed as stated, or it is described as part of what teachers teach.

Vocabulary: Every lesson segment presents words, terms, or phraseology that teachers must teach if students are to understand the content in the lesson segment.

Comprehensibility or Accessibility: This is what the teacher will do to ensure that every student in the room has access to the lesson segment's objective. If second graders are to write a story grammar, it is the teacher's responsibility that the reading and writing demands are within the range of every student in the room, or the teacher makes accommodations to ensure that every student can come away from the lesson with the skills and knowledge the lesson intends for students to have. It is no longer okay for a student to fail to accomplish social studies objectives merely because she does not read or write sufficiently well.

Procedures: This is what the teacher will do to accomplish the objective and ensure comprehensibility or accessibility. Readers should read the procedures section carefully and flesh out the procedures from the brief description offered.

Review and Assessment: Every lesson segment should state its intent (objective) and how the teacher will determine the extent, if any, to which students achieved the objective. Review and assessment can be either formal or informal. However it is done, the teacher needs the students' performance as a guide to inform subsequent instruction.

APPLICATIONS TO THE CLASSROOM

Table 1.1. Sample Lesson Segment, Primary Grades

Objective: Second graders will complete a story grammar for a Founder selected from among resources available in the classroom and the school library. The story grammars will not be longer than one page. The format is included in chapter 3, Biographical Studies.	*Common Core Standard(s)*: Tell a story with appropriate facts and relevant details.

Background: "Yesterday we wrote a story grammar for George Washington and found that in every biography there are characters, settings, problems, and achievements. Today, in partnerships, we will write a story grammar for one of the people whose name is on the board."	*Vocabulary*: *Dyad*: pair *Problem*: obstacles *Achievement*: the result of work and ability *Biography*: story of a person written by another person *Grammar*: taxonomy or system	*Comprehensibility or Accessibility*: Reading and writing tasks are carefully explained to everyone, including the responsibilities of members of each dyad. Less able readers are paired with more able readers. Less able readers dictate sentence ideas to more able readers, who write the sentences on the story grammar format.

Procedures: Having demonstrated story grammar reading and writing on the previous day, teacher reminds pairs of students about how the process works. Each dyad selects a biographical study from the list on the board: John Adams, Thomas Jefferson, Benjamin Franklin, Alexander Hamilton, and James Madison. Each of those is represented in at least one second-grade-reader-friendly reading in print form. In addition, there is Internet access available for each of the five Founders. Students are to name at least two characters, one setting, one problem, and one achievement. The writing is in at least one and not more than two sentences for each of the four sections of the story grammar. The teacher moves around the room answering every question and helping at every opportunity. As students prepare additional story grammars, the teacher slowly and deliberately reduces direct involvement.	*Review and Assessment*: Public reading of story grammars. Comparison of similarities and differences between story grammars written by more than one dyad. "Make a list of what you know about (each of the five biographical subjects)," one at a time. Students' lists should include problems and achievements for at least three of the five biographical subjects.

Table 1.2. Sample Lesson Segment, Intermediate Grades

Objective: Fourth graders will participate in "Read-Write-Share" (see chapter 11: Literacy) to write a biography of a teacher-selected biographical subject. In the fourth grade, biographical subjects could include presidents, inventors, principals in world religions, athletes, writers, musicians, and people of note in other fields. The result of the "Read-Write-Share" activity is discussion of what made the biographical subject notable.	*Common Core Standard(s)*: Paraphrase portions of text read aloud or information presented in diverse media. Report on a topic or text in an organized manner.

Background: "Last week I introduced you to biographies of Ruth Roessel (Navajo), Maria Tallchief (Osage), and Wilma Mankiller (Cherokee). You learned that each of the women is noteworthy in their fields and worthy of study because of their achievements. This week and next week we will read and write about each of them so we can know them in greater detail and understand why they are worthy of our attention."	*Vocabulary*: *Revise*: to change by seeing again *Big Voice*: stronger rather than merely louder *Indian*: native peoples in the Americas *Tribe:* Indian peoples' ancestral groupings	*Comprehensibility or Accessibility*: The read and write sessions are limited to one minute each; for students who do not read and write fluently or well, the wait time is short, so everyone reads and writes as well as possible. Everyone learns most about the biographical subjects by listening. There is far too much back-story to introduce the topic of Indian women. Students get the back-stories by being immersed in the topic and the women's biographies.

Procedures: Begin with a printed biography of Ruth Roessel and follow the "Read-Write-Share" procedures in chapter 11 (Literacy). Biographical materials appear in an Internet search for "Indian women" or "Ruth Roessel." Most of the material is reader-friendly for fourth graders. Teachers may find it helpful to rewrite the biographical material to be even more reader-friendly. Or, the teacher can satisfy the reading portion of the activity by reading aloud and then giving printed material to students to read silently.	*Review and Assessment*: After the session on Ruth Roessel, students volunteer attributes that make her worthy of study. They make lists again after sessions on Maria Tallchief and Wilma Mankiller. Finally, they make a master list of 3-5 attributes common to all of them.

Table 1.3. Sample Lesson Segment, Middle Levels

Objective: Seventh graders will participate in a Speed Bio that produces a biographical focus for each student. Students will select a biographical focus, prepare either synopsis or story grammar, and present the selected biographical focus in a Biographical Roundtable.	*Common Core Standard(s)*: Introduce a topic clearly; organize ideas, concepts, and information; and develop the topic with relevant information and examples.

Background: You recall our work with story grammar and how to write a synopsis or summary. During this period each of us will select someone about whom to write a synopsis or summary, or story grammar, and present our biographical subject in the Biographical Roundtable next Friday. This is one of the several ways we have for biographical study.	*Vocabulary*: *Synopsis or Summary*: Main idea and relevant details *Fluency (writing)*: as much as you can as well as you can *Presentation*: to explain to a group in a manner that the group is likely to find interesting	*Comprehensibility or Accessibility*: Students who struggle with reading will be provided with oral readers and, if necessary, writers to whom the struggling student dictates. During the "Speed Bio," itself, struggling students will read whatever they need in order to make their selection, and they respond to the writing prompts as they are able.

Procedures: Each student has access to five brief biographies from world religions, native peoples, inventors, musicians, and athletes. Most of the brief bios can be taken from the several "100 Most Influential..." books cited in the references in this chapter. Students select one biography from among the five and "read as much as you can as well as you can." At one minute, students write the name of the biographical subject and what appears to be interesting, if anything. They select another and repeat the two notes after one minute. They repeat the process through three biographies, or four, or five. They select one biographical subject from the three to five and prepare either summary or story grammar. Students present their biographical subject in the Biographical Roundtable.	*Review and Assessment*: he teacher keeps account of the biographical presentations on the board, in the five categories. Students receive credit for making a biographical selection, for reading enough to write a summary or story grammar, and for presenting in the Roundtable. In writing, credit is dependent on sentences, relationships between and among sentences, and mechanical control. After the Roundtable, students make lists of biographical subjects they recall and at least one sentence about what they recall about each subject on their list. Content credit goes to a baseline of three subjects (1) to (3) for five or more.

REFERENCES

Collins, Francis S. 2006. *The Language of God: A Scientist Presents Evidence for Belief.* New York: Simon and Schuster.

Common Core State Standards Initiative, June 2, 2010.

Fradin, Dennis B. 1999. *The Signers: The 56 Stories behind the Declaration of Independence.* New York: Walker and Company.

———. 2005. *The Founders: The 39 Stories behind the United States Constitution.* New York: Walker and Company.

Hart, Michael H. 1978. *The 100: A Ranking of the Most Influential Persons in History.* Secaucus, NJ: Citadel Press.

Harvey, Sheridan. 2001. *American Women: A Library of Congress Guide for the Study of Woman's History and Culture in the United States.* Washington, DC: Library of Congress.

Hook, Sidney. 1992. *The Hero in History: A Study in Limitation and Possibility.* New Brunswick, NJ: Transaction.

Kansas Curricular Standards for Civics, Government, Economics, Geography, and History, July 1999.

King, Barbara J. 2002. *Biological Anthropology: An Evolutionary Perspective.* CD Series, Chantilly, VA: The Teaching Company.

Knauer, Kelly, ed. 1999. *Time 100: Builders and Titans, Great Minds of the Century.* New York: Time Books.

Krull, Kathleen. 1993. *Lives of the Musicians: Good Times, Bad Times (And What the Neighbors Thought).* San Diego: Harcourt, Brace and Company.

Lossing, Barbara J. (1848) 2004. *Signers of the Declaration of Independence.* Aledo, TX: WallBuilders.

Meyer, Nicilas E. 2001. *Biographical Dictionary of Hispanic Americans.* 2nd ed. New York: Checkmark Books.

Murray, Peter. 2005. *The Most Influential People of the Last 100 Years.* Old Saybrook, CT: Konecky and Konecky.

Salley, Columbus. 1999. *The Black 100: A Ranking of the Most Influential African Americans, Past and Present.* Secaucus, NJ: Carol Publishing Group.

Simmons, John. 1996. *The Scientific 100: A Ranking of the Most Influential Scientists, Past and Present.* New York: Kensington.

CHAPTER 2

History

The United States and the World

There are about as many commentaries about history as there are people who make commentaries about history. Henry Ford said history is bunk. John Gardner said history never looks like history when you're living through it. Real history looks messy, and it feels uncomfortable. Someone said that history repeats itself, and someone else said the only reason history repeats itself is because people don't pay attention the first time. James Loewin tells us history teachers lie to their students, and Howard Zinn says that the historical record changes with the perspective of the historian.

We cannot teach history well if we do not know *what* we are teaching. *What* we are teaching is at least as important as *how* we teach it, and arguably more. We know *what* we are teaching when we teach reading, for example, because five decades ago we started looking at what good readers do when they read, and we use that analysis to inform reading instruction.

Some areas of the curriculum do not enjoy the evidence-based content stability that reading has achieved. Students' writing performance, for example, reflects terrific instruction in the wrong content.

Sometimes, the profession has a reasonable perspective on content that has not yet permeated routine instruction. A case in point is geography, which is mostly locational in schools where geography is taught at all. But perspectives on content in geography have been expanded to reflect a content range far broader than where places are. There is an entire chapter in this book about geography in which locations represent but one of six patterns of geographic content. What about history?

THE CONTENT FOR TEACHING HISTORY

Our reading of Barton (2008, 239–58) suggests there may be six patterns of content for history instruction: knowing about the past, the narrative form, using evidence to inform and to explain, understanding perspectives, interpreting, and generalizing.

Many people, when asked about their experience with history, self-report that it is boring. But history is thrilling, not boring. What can be boring is history instruction, and history instruction is boring when it fails to notice the point of history. The point is stories of people whose meanderings through the ages left footprints (literally in some cases) for us to read and come slowly to inferential understanding of who they were and who we have been.

History is not tables of contents in history textbooks. Those are merely convenient segments for six-week grading periods. History has meaning when we decide what its content is. We need to see everything through the lens of what history *is*. We have to read every history lesson plan and "best practices" book through the critical lens that asks, "Is this history?"

The history we live is more interesting than chronological entries in history books' tables of contents. What is history? It is interesting.

It is common to read and hear forms of Santayana's statement, "Those who cannot remember the past are condemned to repeat it" (1905, 28). Hegel's observation, "We learn from history that we do not learn from history" is a variation on Santayana's theme. Another is that the problem isn't that we do not learn from history; rather, it is that we fail to pay attention. History is a warning.

What is history? Perhaps we begin with Mark Twain, who remarks, "The very ink with which history is written is merely fluid prejudice," where *prejudice* is to *pre judge*. History is people's view of things. History is perspective. Twain's quote characterizes history as people's values and attitudes, that history is shaded by the way people are inclined to understand what they see and hear and, therefore, what they say and write. We need to understand that, *prejudice* is a reflection of who we are when we write and read history.

Schweikart and Allen (2004), professors of history at University of Dayton and University of Washington, respectively, wrote *A Patriot's History of the United States*. They openly acknowledge that their effort is an attempt to counter the "people's" perspective of U.S. history promulgated in, for example, *A People's History of the United States* (Zinn 1980). The merits of the two history books are not important here. That there are two history books of such dramatic difference is important here. What is history? It is a reflection of the historian who writes it. Winston Churchill observed, "History will be kind to me for I intend to write it." He did, and it is.

If history were "bunk," as Henry Ford called it, or lies as James Loewin (1995) suggests, or merely perspective, as Howard Zinn says, why not just be upfront with our students and tell them that what they are reading is merely a history writer's perspective?

If Ambrose Bierce is right about history when he observes that it is "An account, mostly false, of events unimportant, which are brought about by rulers, mostly knaves, and soldiers, mostly fools"; it would appear to any sensible reader that we waste our students' time trying to teach them that history matters.

What we have to do is help students understand that history is a narrative construction of inferences drawn from best evidence (Collingwood 1965, xv), about times, peoples, and events; not the whole story of any event or any one people or any time (Levstik and Barton 2005, 7). History could not be a whole story of anything, as E. H. Carr realized that what he thought might be a complete history of Greece during the period of the Persian wars was not only selections of historians' perceptions, but narratives that lacked the stories of nearly everyone who lived in that period and whose observations were never consulted (Carr 1961).

History is a story of war in Southeast Asia, not an exact narrative of everything and everyone associated with that war in Southeast Asia (Lerner 1997, 204). It is also not the story of the whole war because K–12 textbooks include not a single mention of Gene, a Navy SEAL, who was there and participated valiantly, but his story was unknown until it appeared in *Men in Green Faces* (Wentz and Jurus 1992). When we read as many as a dozen histories of the United States' war in Southeast Asia and never read of Gene, whatever history we read is incomplete. If we do not teach the fundamental idea of incompleteness when we teach history, whatever else we teach about history is compromised by its absence.

Furthermore, it isn't this or that perspective on history that matters. But the idea of perspective, itself, certainly does matter. The idea of history as inquiry matters. Inquiry about the past matters. Consequences matter. Curiosity—the foundation of inquiry—matters. Inferential thinking matters. The questions that lead to understanding Alexander, Genghis Khan, and Leonardo da Vinci, in their geographic, economic, and cultural contexts, matter. It may not matter so much who fought and who prevailed in a war among ourselves in the United States in the middle of the nineteenth century, but it matters that there was such a war and why, and what consequences of that war bear on how we think and feel and live to this day.

We cannot dismiss the existence of historical information, because the inferences, perspectives, and inquiries associated with history have to come from something and "hang" on something. We cannot say that the best factual evidence does not matter, that meanings and inferences are all that matter, because the meanings and inferences are made of the best factual evidence. There are two questions here, both of which bear on what we teach when we think we are teaching history. One, what is "best factual evidence?" In history, it is whatever historians decide to give credence. Facts, as Carr writes, do not speak for themselves; facts speak only when historians call on them to speak, and the meanings they speak depend entirely on how historians decide to use them (Carr 1961, 9).

Two, how does a person or an event become "best factual historical evidence"? It isn't that something is a fact in history because it happened. If that were the case, it would be impossible to find enough paper on which to write all the facts of history, for everything that ever happened would be a fact, including that a woman named Begay made mutton stew on Tuesday, March 14, 1846, over a fire beside her makeshift shelter near Fort Defiance. We know it happened, whether or not it was recorded, because she was one of thousands of people like her who camped at Fort Defiance during those dreadful days of the Navajo's Long Walk, and she would have been one of scores of women who made mutton stew to feed her family. But she is not a fact of history because she was never recorded. The absence of a record that can be verified means only that she did not leave one.

Caesar's crossing of an insignificant little body of running water also happened, as did the crossing of that River Rubicon by tens of thousands of people both before there was a Caesar and in the hundreds of years since. But Caesar's crossing of the Rubicon is recorded as history of the day. To be evidence, events and people have to have been recorded. Clearly, evidence is selected, for no one records every occurrence. The historical record is an accumulation of selected occurrences, and history is the narrative that puts the selected occurrences in order and makes them readable. That is what history is, and that is what our students must come to understand.

There is one additional part of this discussion of origins in the nature of history, and it is crucial to our own and our students' understanding of what history is. The record that makes Caesar's crossing of the Rubicon historical evidence was not written by "winners" in particular, or even "winners" in general. It was written by people who write. Cherokees, for example, are among the most recognized native peoples in the United States, and anyone familiar with the Trail of Tears knows that Cherokees did not win that one. But they recorded it, in their Cherokee language. Win or lose, the record is everything.

History is a narrative wrapped around selected occurrences made evidential because they have been recorded and can be verified. History is also like science (Collingwood 1956). It is about questions. It is far more like a way of thinking than a body of knowledge.

History, like science, is messy, confusing, and uncomfortable, mostly because it keeps changing. It doesn't change from inaccurate to accurate; it changes from what we thought we knew to what we have to think about in light of new questions. Like science, it is rarely entirely wrong. It was just incomplete, or more accurately, rested on information that was half wrong. Historians, like scientists, near-always work with information that is partly wrong. The problem is that they don't know how much of which part is wrong. To be historically literate, our students have to understand that relationship between history and science.

However, there are some things we do know, and this much is probably correct.

One, because history is more a way of thinking than a body of knowledge, it does not exist in tables of contents in history texts.

Two, children think historically at a very young age (Barton 2008, 239).

Three, whatever history we were taught when we were in K–12 school was almost certainly not as accurate as our teachers suggested, or insisted. But if they are to blame for anything, it is that they didn't teach us that science and history are equally messy.

Four, the historian wasn't there, and whoever wrote what the historian is depending on was not necessarily any more dependable for unfiltered truth than anyone else is, or has ever been.

Five, history is not a neat portfolio of information that can be committed to a list of grade level exit competencies or understandings. Like science, history is also not "a system that steadily advances toward a state of finality" (Popper 1959); rather, history is guided by guesses that can lead to discoveries.

Six, while history appears linear, in that things happen in what is, after the fact, a sequence, learning to think historically is at least as much perpendicular as it is horizontal. To understand the revolution that eventuated in the United States of America requires that students learn about the one in Russia in the early twentieth century and eventuated in the Soviet Union (or was that a civil war?), the one in England in the seventeenth and eighteenth centuries (which is called a civil war), the one in Cuba in the middle of the twentieth century (which is called a revolution but was largely Cuban against Cuban), and the one in China in the first half of the twentieth century that eventuated in the People's Republic of China (and was Chinese against Chinese, as well). The history lesson is the idea of revolution; George Washington, the Delaware River, Valley Forge, Dorchester Heights, and Trenton are merely pieces in an ideational fabric.

When we help our students weave the fabric and include geography, biology, and music in the weave, they start to understand something of history. But is there time for that grand weaving project? We have thirteen years.

What is the content of history for our purposes as social studies teachers in K–8 classrooms? What do we teach when we think we are teaching history?

1. We teach that history is an incomplete story about people, places, and events.
2. We teach that every story has consequences.
3. We teach that history is told from a variety of perspectives.
4. We teach that the history our students learn reflects what historians have decided merits the name "history."
5. We teach that the facts of history exist as facts because historians have decided to give more credence to some people and events than to other people and events. The people and events to which historians have decided to give special credence are what we refer to as the facts of history.
6. We teach our students to pose history questions. On what basis (or bases) are selections of facts made? Who decides what history is in our textbook? Who determines what is important to include on history tests?

7. We teach them that they cannot think historically if they do not have the perpendicular and the horizontal timelines, and the colors. The more historical knowledge they have, the more they can learn from any historical information posed (Collingwood 1956, 247).
8. We teach them that history is a study of details and big pictures and that they are responsible for weaving big pictures that make sense to them.

Where does all that leave us? We want to teach our students the truth, at least the closest we can come to an accurate approximation of truth. However, it is rarely possible to be absolutely sure of what is true, certainly as the past gets further and further away from the verifiable record. We might refer to the problem as *responsible subjectivity*, wherein we know that the history we teach is the best approximation of truth we can manage, and we (teachers) are aware of similar and inevitable limitations, even in science.

Mostly, we want to teach how people can accumulate historical information relevant to their construction of responsible approximations of truth. We don't teach James Loewin or Howard Zinn as alternative truths; we teach Loewin, Zinn, and Schweikart and Allen, because they all show that history demands of students and their teachers a good measure of the skepticism that starts *inquiry*.

We could begin the inquiry with who wrote the fifth grade history book. Who published it, who sits on the publisher's board of directors? If the publisher is part of a conglomerate, what else does the conglomerate do? Where does the author teach? What does the author teach?

Perhaps students should prepare a letter of inquiry to the editor of their textbook. Perhaps they write to the editor and ask for the publisher's "author guide" or "spec sheet." They might ask the editor if the author was directed to emphasize, or deemphasize, any historical perspective. Students might ask the author if the proposal review process dictated any changes in the history the author wrote in the book proposal. They could ask if the book is an argument, an inquiry, or just scissors and paste (Collingwood 1956, 257).

TWO KINDS OF HISTORY

History is often written as an argument. For example, there has been a pervading question about whether Europeans were, in general, or Columbus was, in particular, the first explorer of what became the New World. Menzies (2003) found a map dated 1424 and signed by its Venetian cartographer, Zuane Pizzigano, that showed perfectly accurate coastlines for Europe. There were also four islands shown in the Western Atlantic, the opposite side of the Atlantic Ocean from Portugal. The largest island of the four had towns marked. Further study suggested the only plausible conclusion—the islands were modern-day Puerto Rico and Guadeloupe. As a result of the map, Menzies wrote an argument that someone reached the Caribbean and established a colony sixty-eight years before Columbus arrived (Menzies 2003, 31).

Bengtsson argues that "Vikings peopled Iceland in 860 and Greenland in 986" (1954, xvii). Mowat (2002) made the argument that there is evidence of European exploration of the Americas perhaps hundreds of years prior to Columbus.

Mowat found three cairns (rock piles), cylindrical and about six feet high, that are unlike anything Eskimo inuksuak (stone men) across the Arctic ever constructed. The thickness of the lichen growth on them, Mowat wrote, is too old to belong to the Eskimoan period (2002, 6). There is a sort of broad pathway or ramp running seaward from the high tide line. Somebody had put in a lot of work clearing it of the worst of its jagged rocks. No Eskimo would go to that much trouble to make a boat landing for their small kayaks and canoes. "This must have been a haul-out for big boats, Mowat quoted Thomas Lee, archaeologist from Queen's Laval University (2002, 7).

What is the historical argument? Europeans, Asians, or at least peoples who favored big boats, as Arctic natives did not, were in the Americas at least as many as six hundred years before Columbus, and some may not have been Vikings.

History is also crafted as inquiry, with questions, hypotheses, and the requirement of replicable evidence. Jared Diamond, a biologist, was walking along a Papua, New Guinea, beach one day, talking with Yali, a local politician. Yali peppered the conversation with questions, always friendly and invariably penetrating. Among the questions Yali asked was, "Why is it that you white people developed so much cargo [New Guinean term for modern goods] and brought it to New Guinea, but we black people had little cargo of our own?" (Diamond 1999, 14). The question stayed with Diamond for twenty-five years. *Guns, Germs, and Steel* is his answer to Yali's question.

Yali's question, and Diamond's search followed in a general sense the process of science. Diamond (1999, 405–25) answered Yali's question in his epilogue: "the striking differences between the long-term histories of peoples of different continents have been due not to innate differences in the peoples themselves but to differences in their environments" (405). The rest of the epilogue is a description of how scientific methods influence how historians construct history.

The construction material for both argument and inquiry is historical instances, arrangements of which represent lines of evidence. Eskimoan peoples, it was argued, had no reason to build landings for big boats. Who did have such reason? In the year 800, Charlemagne spent time on the Channel (eventually named English Channel) overseeing a boat-building project for the purpose of challenging raids from Denmark (Wilson 2005, 79). Those Danes were part of people we know as Vikings. The fleet-building being overseen by Charlemagne was French, or English, not Viking.

Who built those ships and sailed them to the Arctic region? Vikings, perhaps, but the builders and sailors may have been forbearers of the French and English.

How Charlemagne spent a portion of the year 800 adds to a line of evidence that responds to the question of who built the big boats that needed the landings that Farley Mowat found in the modern Arctic.

THREE BELIEF SYSTEMS ABOUT TEACHING HISTORY

There appear to be three general perspectives on history content. Remember that what we teach is a reflection of what we believe, our responsible subjectivity. People who teach history, therefore, tend to reflect one or some combination of three perspectives on content.

One, some people think American history can be either critical or patriotic (Burack, J., 3-6-2006, H-High-S@H-Net.MSU.EDU, a listserv for teaching social studies in secondary schools). Is history supposed to be "critical"? "Patriotic"?

What would "critical" history look like? People who think and teach at the critical end of the line might suggest we read *A People's History for the Classroom* (Bigelow 2008). History from a critical perspective is founded on a contrary principle. We read about Pa and that good bottomland he found on the trek west, looking for a place to settle down and make a home for the family. Critical history is about to whom that good bottomland belongs. Critical history refers to the Westward Movement as invasion.

Critical history asks how Thomas Jefferson could draft that fine prose about all men being created equal, even as he owned some of those men and women. Critical history acknowledges the Henry Ford dynasty and how it changed the world of transportation, and it asks about the people who stood at the assembly line that Ford created.

While more traditional (patriotic) biographies of Columbus tell of the heroic exploration, critical history tells of what Columbus left behind after his third voyage. Critical history does not deny much of traditional (patriotic) perspectives on history, but it does stand up and say, "Wait a minute! There is a whole lot more to this story."

What would "patriotic" history look like? Just as we started with Bigelow's *People's History* as a foundation for critical history, we start with Schweikart and Allen's *Patriot's History* as an alternative to critical history. Schweikart and Allen observe that "compared with any other nation in the world, America's past is a bright and shining light" (2004, xi). They reflect Churchill's observation that America's government is the worst possible, except for all the rest.

A patriot's history emphasizes the bright and shining light. It does not deny that Jefferson's slaves labored on his plantation; rather it emphasizes the marvelous prose he composed for the nation's Declaration of Independence, his responsibility for establishing the great University of Virginia, and his presidency during which the landmass of the growing country was doubled with the addition of his Louisiana Purchase.

Patriotic history acknowledges that all men in fact were not created equal in those early days of the republic, that the prose was symbolic of an ideal, an ideal that was eventually fulfilled because the founders made a nation that could make it so. Patriotic history records Tom Brokaw's *The Greatest Generation* (2004) as part of "Democracy's Finest Hour" (Schweikart and Allen 2004, chapter 17).

Patriotic history is neither true nor untrue. It is a way of looking at the content we teach. It isn't different history content from critical history; it emphasizes the content differently. Zinn acknowledged his different emphasis in his *People's History of the United States*. He did not change the content; he merely emphasized the content differently, as do Schweikart and Allen.

The question here is not whether there are two different ways to emphasize the record. The question is whether either or both of the emphases promulgate a political purpose. We have a professional responsibility to ask whether there is a place in the social studies for instruction with a political purpose, where students are a captive audience and the teacher holds an enormous power advantage.

A second belief system among history teachers features another dichotomy of focus. On one side, teachers (and professors and textbook writers) believe that history instruction should be "issues-based," that is, anchored in conflicts and controversies. The purpose of teaching history from an issues-based perspective is to engage students in the conflicts and controversies so they come to appreciate conflicting perspectives in history. On the other side, teachers, professors, and textbook writers believe that history should be content-based, that is, anchored in what we know and what the record shows about how history played out over the years.

Issues-based social studies instruction identifies a controversy, perhaps freedom of access to public accommodations. That one loomed large in 1960 when four black college students walked into a "five and dime" store in Greensboro, North Carolina, bought school supplies, and sat at the lunch counter. It was a segregated lunch counter, and they were not served. They sat, unserved, until the store closed and they were forced to leave.

The lunch counter at the "five and dime" was a public accommodation. The issue involves the law, the Constitution, people's rights, property rights, legal segregation, even the extent to which black people have the right to the essence of full citizenship in the constitutional republic. Studying the issue requires that students become sufficiently literate in the laws of the time that affected the issue. They also need to come to know the history, the social structures, the distinction between human rights and property rights, and what "citizenship" means.

There is also a content-based instructional perspective on social studies, in this case history. Content instruction does not ignore the issues; it emphasizes the nature of history so students have the tools with which to use historical analyses to understand the issues. Issues-based social studies (history in this case) begins with issues and assumes content development wherefrom; content-based social studies begins with the content and assumes the skills to engage in issues. Issues-based social studies emphasizes the emergence of content through the study of the big pictures. Content-based social studies emphasizes the emergence of big pictures through the study of history and interrelationships among the other social studies and the larger curriculum.

A third dichotomy in history is anchoring it in events, or anchoring it in people. The former think history is about what happened, as close as can be determined by listening to and observing those who were as close as possible to being there at the time (primary sources). The latter think history is the people who made it, as close as possible to knowing through the voices of those who recorded the words and deeds (primary sources) of movers and shakers. The latter tend toward a vision of history made by people. The former tends away from people and toward how events affected people.

History as the study of people cuts a wide swath. It accommodates any of the perspectives on history in this chapter, whether patriotic or critical, issues-based or content-based. The selection of biographical subjects can skew the study of history in any direction (patriotic or critical).

An event-oriented history is also vulnerable to the effects of selection, but the events tend to be relatively standardized. American history will include major wars (French and Indian, Revolution, War of 1812, Civil, Spanish American, and World Wars I and II). There are also the ages and nonmilitary revolutions (Industrial, Atomic, Technological, and so forth), major topics (slavery, Westward Movement, Indian Removal, immigration, Depression), certain "movements" (women's, civil rights, Red Scare), and iconic people (Patrick Henry, Abraham Lincoln, Theodore Roosevelt, Franklin Roosevelt, Rosa Parks, Martin Luther King Jr.). Any review of most history texts will show wars, ages, topics, movements, and iconic people in greater frequency than just about anything else.

HISTORY AS SCALE

There are two primary problems that make history especially complex among other content in the comprehensive curriculum. One, most students haven't prior knowledge for much of what we teach when we teach history. History instruction, therefore, demands that teachers teach the prior knowledge required for the history content they intend to teach.

The U.S. Religious Knowledge Survey (2010), for example, reveals that average Americans do not know very much of their own religion and considerably less about other people's religions. Middle school teachers cannot teach the foundations of Abrahamic religions to students who do not bring knowledge of Abraham and his wife, Sarah, and their three sons, all crucial in very different ways to the three Abrahamic religions. Teachers responsible for instruction in world religions have to teach basic prior knowledge before they can teach histories, geographies, and biographies in three major world religions.

The other problem is about scale. Everything we teach is too far, too long ago, or too big. Primary students cannot conceptualize two hundred years ago, or twenty, for that matter. They love prehistoric reptiles, but they have no sense of their time. A million is too many. A world war is too big. So much of what we have to teach is too distant for our students to access. We know that many students cannot conceptualize much of what we teach, but we teach the events anyway and hope our students can wrap their minds around the time problem eventually. Perhaps it is a matter of scale.

Bill Bryson is a terrific vignette-teller. In his *A Short History of Nearly Everything* (2003), he explains things of enormous size, distance, and time. He uses scale. For example, most of us cannot conceptualize the 4.5 billion years that constitute Earth's age or even the 6 or 7 million years since bipedal mammals started to move about (King 2002). He poses a situation that finds us flying back in time at a rate of one year per second. At that rate, we would get to the time of Christ in about thirty minutes, several months to get to the beginnings of human life, and twenty years to get to the beginnings of the Cambrian period. "It was, in other words, an extremely long time ago, and the world was a very different place." (Bryson 2003, 325).

The appearance of human beings (homo erectus) in the 4.5 billion years of the planet's existence is difficult for most of us to conceptualize. Bryson tells us to stretch our arms out from our sides as far as possible. "On this scale," he writes, "all of complex life is in the most recent hand (wrist to fingertips), and with a single stroke of a medium-grained nail file you could eradicate human history" (Bryson 2003, 337).

We need to understand that we teach about Indian people at and immediately following European arrival and expansion. We teach the growth of cities and communication technology. We teach the era of the U.S. Constitution and the Declaration of Independence. We teach about the origins of Judaism, Christianity, Islam, Buddhism, and Hinduism. We teach Alexander the Great, Plato, Abraham Lincoln, and George Washington.

How do we help fifth graders understand 150 years ago (U.S. Civil War) when their active memories are under eleven years, they think their thirty-year-old parents lived in the old days, and their fifty-five-year-old grandparents are ancient?

It is possible that students will understand the history we teach when we begin teaching the content of history, just as we have with reading. We do not teach reading; we teach word attack and comprehension, engagement in text, and what it means to come away from text with some of the text stuck in our minds. We do not teach history; we teach content and controversies, people and events, facts and possibilities, inquiry and skepticism. We teach how to think like historians, because we understood what that means, and we remember our teachers who taught that history, and those who did not.

APPLICATIONS TO THE CLASSROOM

Table 2.1 Sample Lesson Segment, Primary Grades

Objective: First graders will be able to place the birthdays of each student in the class on a timeline divided in twelve one-month segments. The lesson sets a stage for both horizontal and perpendicular historical thinking.	*State Social Studies Standard(s)*: Most states show standards that "develop and understand timelines" (Florida), "family timeline" (New York), and "a child's place in time and space" (Ohio). The CCS do not show history standards for primary grades.

Background: Most of us have different birthdays. Most of our birthdays come during one year. We are going to see the one-year during which we have birthdays, and we are going to see where our birthday is on a chart that shows everyone's birthdays.	*Vocabulary*: *Timeline*: chart that shows history as time with events and people in periods. *Horizontal*: straight line that connects left and right *Perpendicular*: straight line that connects up and down by going through a horizontal line	*Comprehensibility or Accessibility*: There is nothing to read or write in this lesson, and the only term that is remotely important is *timeline*, and that will become clear as we use one for their own birthdays. The teacher will use *horizontal* and *perpendicular* in natural discussion during the several days of preparation of the timeline, but there will be no demand that first graders use those two terms. Many will, but it is not required.

Procedures: Show a long (3' – 5') horizontal line on the board. Divide the line into twelve equal parts, and label each part with the months of the year. Call the timeline by name. Solicit the name of today's month (September). Ask if anyone has a birthday in September. Write one of the volunteering student's name on the timeline at September. If there are two, write the name above the first name and call the placement by name: "I will write Rhoda's name above Emilio's name. That starts a perpendicular line at September. I wonder if there will be more perpendicular lines (make your hand go up and down) on our horizontal timeline (make your hand go left and right) line this year. We will just have to see." Solicit birthdays for October, and record it (or them) on the timeline, and use the vocabulary. Two months is enough for the first day. Record two months per day until the timeline is complete.	*Review and Assessment*: "Look at our history of birthdays." Whose birthday comes first, the earliest? Whose birthday is the latest? Which month has the most birthdays? Which month has the biggest perpendicular line? "I wonder of we could put my birthday on the timeline." The discussion moves to what to do when we have to use years instead of months to record birthdays.

Table 2.2. Sample Lesson Segment, Intermediate Grades

Objective: Sixth graders will write autobiography as history, thinking throughout that what they write today can be primary source material for historians in ages far into the future. Student autobiographers will record many names and some people's stories to provide the texture for historical narratives.	*Common Core Standard(s)*: Write narratives to develop real or imagined experiences.

Background: What if you found a box in your attic that contained a diary written by your grandmother or grandfather when they were in the sixth grade almost 100 years ago? Would you want to read their history? What if the diary you found were from your grandmother's grandmother, or her grandmother, or her grandmother? Let's calculate how old that last diary might be. We are going to write a kind of diary that could last that long.	*Vocabulary*: *Autobiography*: We write our own story. *Biography*: Someone else writes our story. *Generation*: By our definition, a generation is 25 years. *Primary Source*: Source material that is closest as possible to the person or event being described.	*Comprehensibility or Accessibility*: We have all known other people. There are very few organic or functional limitations that interfere with a 12-year-old's memory of his or her friends. Very few twelve year olds are unable to use a keyboard to record their thoughts. For the most inconvenienced students, the teacher will open a desktop file and tutor those students in making a list of names.

Procedures: Write the names of the people who came to our last birthday. Write each person's last name comma and first name. Each time you write a name, put in alphabetical order. Write the names of the people you know from Sunday school, musical instrument lessons, and sports practice. Write the names of everyone you remember from the third and fourth grades. Write the names of everyone you know who can speak more than one language. When your list shows at least ten names, before adding more names, pick one name and write a sentence after his or her name that how you know the person. For the next two weeks, we will list names and write sentences after as many names as we can to show who they are and how we know them. To show who they are and how we know them, we will have to write at least two sentences for each name we chose to write about.	*Review and Assessment*: After two weeks, the teacher will conduct conferences with each student, three per day all students have engaged in conference. The teacher will read from the screen and make recommendations about sentence-writing and, if necessary, plan a lesson or two about thinking and writing in the kinds of sentences this activity demands. The teacher will look for evidence of participation (length of lists. Conferences will inform follow-up.

Table 2.3 Sample Lesson Segment, Middle Levels

Objective: Given a close reading of a selected page of the textbook, students will be able to participate in text-dependent questions regarding the hunter-gatherer lifestyle. The teacher will expand on the textbook's narrative with information that distinguishes among hominids who represent the hunter-gatherer period (4,000,000 years): Astralopithecus afarensis, Homo habilis, Homo erectus, Neandertal, Homo sapien. The timeline and terminology from biological anthropology are included for purposes of extended knowledge only.	*Common Core Standards*: Cite textual evidence to support analysis of what text says. Develop a theme or central idea of a text.

Background: The reading and questions focus on cause and effect relationships. That means that one or more things (cause) can be connected to something else (effect). A hurricane, for example, is a cause; flooding and wind damage are effects connected to the cause. The damage comes directly from the hurricane.	*Vocabulary*: *Biological anthropology*: study of genetic and behavioral variation among, in this case, bipedal hominids *Homo*: Latin for the genus in which several species occur *Afarensis*: Latin for the species we know as hominid *Taxonomy*: system for grouping, biology	*Comprehensibility or Accessibility*: Close reading increases the probability of comprehension, especially for readers who struggle to construct meaning from text. With regard to taxonomic information in biological anthropology, the teacher will place the hominids along a timeline to provide context, and use extended arm length to scale the timeline.

Procedures: We are going to close-read a passage from the textbook's narrative on prehistorical hominids (humans) during the 4,000,000 years of the hunter-gatherer period. I will ask you text-dependent questions about cause and effects relationships between how Paleolithic hunter-gatherers lived and where they lived. Teacher will review close-reading procedures. In dyads, review conversation frame as prelude to translating the text passage into their own words. Teacher reads text passage aloud, and goes to discussion of why hunter-gatherers could not live sedentary life style. Students summarize text passage.	*Review and Assessment*: Review translations and summaries. Begin to complete the cause-effect chart that begins with hunting and gathering and leads to invention of agriculture.

REFERENCES

Barton, Keith C. 2008. "Research on Students' Ideas about History." In *Handbook of Research in Social Studies Education*, edited by Linda S. Levstik and Cynthia A. Tyson. New York: Routledge.

Bengtsson, Francis G. 1954. *The Long Ships*. New York: New York Review of Books.

Bigelow, Bill. 2008. *A People's History for the Classroom*. Milwaukee, WI: Rethinking Schools.

Brokaw, Tom. 2004. *The Greatest Generation*. New York: Random House.

Bryson, Bill. 2003. *A Short History of Nearly Everything*. New York: Broadway Books.

Carr, Edward, H. 1961. *What Is History?* New York: Vintage Books.

Collingwood, Robert G. 1956. *The Idea of History*. London: Oxford University Press.

Diamond, Jared. 1999. *Guns, Germs, and Steel: The Fates of Human Societies*. New York: W.W. Norton.

King, Barbara J. 2002. *Biological Anthropology: An Evolutionary Perspective*. CD Series. Chantilly, VA: The Teaching Company.

Lerner, Gerda. 1997. *Why History Matters: Life and Thought*. New York: Oxford University Press.

Levstik, Linda S., and Keith C. Barton. 2005. *Doing History: Investigating with Children in Elementary and Middle Schools*. Mahwah, NJ: Lawrence Erlbaum Publishers.

Loewin, James. 1995. *Lies My Teacher Told Me: Everything Your American History Teacher Got Wrong*. New York: Touchstone.

Menzies, Gavin. 2003. *1421: The Year China Discovered America*. New York: Perennial.

Mowat, Farley. 2002. *The Farfarers: Before the Norse*. Toronto, Canada: Anchor Canada.

Popper, Sir Karl. 1959. *The Logic of Scientific Discovery*. New York: Basic Books. In *Science Says: A Collection of Quotations in the History, Meaning, and Practice of Science*, edited by Robert Kaplan, 48. New York: W. H. Freeman.

Santayana, George. 1905. *The Life of Reason*. Vol. 1. New York: Prometheus Books.

Schweikart, Larry, and Michael Allen. 2004. *A Patriot's History of the United States*. New York: Penguin Group.

The Pew Forum on Religion and Public Life. U.S. Religious Knowledge Survey. 2010. www.pewforum.org/U-S-Religious-Knowledge-Survey.aspx.

Wentz, Gene, and Betty A. Jurus. 1992. *Men in Green Faces*. New York: St. Martin's Press.

Wilson, Derek. 2005. *Charlemagne: A Biography*. New York: Vintage Books.

Zinn, Howard. 2003. *A People's History of the United States*. New York: HarperCollins.

CHAPTER 3

World Religions

Monday School, Not Sunday School

This chapter distinguishes between Monday-Tuesday-Wednesday-Thursday-Friday, between about 8:00 a.m. and 3:00 p.m. (Monday school), and Saturday-Sunday all day (Sunday school). On weekdays, before about 8:00 a.m. and after about 3:00 p.m. and on Saturdays and Sundays, students are with families, friends, and en route to school.

With regard to matters of faith, any and all matters associated in any way with religion have their place on Saturdays, Sundays, and at the family dinner table. For many reasons, not the least of which is the First Amendment to the U.S. Constitution, matters of religious faith are private communications between each student and his family and, if any, with people in the family's place of worship. That is nonnegotiable.

To make clear the hard distinction between Sunday school and Monday school, consider several quotations from one resource that reveals many contrasts. The back cover of Francis S. Collins's book reads, in part, "Dr. Francis Collins, head of the Human Genome Project, is one of the world's leading scientists. He works at the cutting edge of the study of DNA, the code of life. Yet he is also a man of unshakable faith in God and scripture" (Collins 2006).

The phrases on both sides of the following t-chart come from several places in Collins's book. Numerals in parentheses indicate page numbers in his book, *The Language of God*. In some instances (the first two phrases and the second two phrases, numbered three), the phrase on the right finishes the sentence started on the left. Thus, "We have caught the first glimpse of our own instruction book" appears on Collins's page three as the beginning of a sentence; "previously known only to God" finishes that sentence. It is verifiably true that the Human Genome Project reveals how our genetic makeup is designed, and we have never known that before. The opening clause is science, and it belongs in Monday school. The end of that sentence reads, "previously known only to God" is a reference to a concept of omniscience, omnipresence, and omnipotence that rests on faith, and it belongs in Sunday school.

Matters of verifiable science belong in Monday school. Matters of faith belong in Sunday school. God (name, title, ever-present, all-powerful, all-moral, father in heaven, monotheistic father, creator of the universe, existence before the Big Bang, man's rule-giver, holy spirit, greatest of all mechanical engineers, supreme intelligence, and other variations on the theme) is Sunday school. Biology is Monday school. Natural selection is Monday school. An earth that began in 4004 BCE is Sunday school.

On the surface, the book of Genesis is Sunday school. But as a history of the first 4,000 years of human civilization (Asimov 1969, 7), it can be Monday school, and Asimov points out the distinction between the historical Genesis and the scholarly history in the modern sense. Genesis can be cultural history, which would make it Monday school. If Genesis is taught as a poem, and the literacy ob-

Table 3.1.   Distinctions between Monday School and Sunday School

MONDAY SCHOOL	SUNDAY SCHOOL
"We have caught the first glimpse of our own instruction book…" (3)	",,, previously known only to God." (3)
"… a stunning scientific achievement…" (3)	"… and an occasion of worship." (3)
"Science is the only reliable way to understand the natural world (6).	"But science is powerless to answer the questions such as Why did the university come into being? What is the meaning of human existence? What happens after we die'?" (6)
"The universe is approximately 14.6 billion years old." (88)	"Could there be a more important question in all of human existence than 'Is there a God'?" (20)
"… an age of Earth of 4.55 billion years (89)	
"Evolution, as a mechanism, can be and must be true." (107)	"But that says nothing about the nature of its author." (107)
"By DNA analysis, we humans are truly part of one family"(bipedal hominids). (126)	"The DNA sequence evidence, powerful though it is (127) "…does not tell us what it means to be human." (140)
Begin with human DNA sequence. What is the likelihood of finding a *similar* DNA sequence in genomes of other organisims? Chimpanzee (100%), Dog (99%), Mouse (99%), Chicken (75%), Fruit Fly (60%), Round Worm (35%). (127)	"I do not feel obligated to believe that the same God who endowed us with sense, reason, and intellect has intended us to forego its use." – Galileo (in Collins (158)

jective is to understand the forms in which poetry can appear, it is Monday school. As the story of Hebrews' god, the creator, it is Sunday school.

Bishop Ussher is Monday school. William Paley is Monday school. Mohammad is Monday school. Jesus Christ, John Calvin, Siddhartha Gautama, Abraham, St. Augustine, and Maimonides are Monday school. Those people can be verified. They are biographical studies as content in the study of world religions.

Just because someone is a major figure in the context of world religions does not mean he or she is Sunday school. Sarah and Khadijah were wives of Abraham and Muhammad, respectively. That they appear in the Old and New Testaments of the Bible and in the Quran, respectively, do not make them solely Sunday school topics. We can teach and learn about each of them as significant people in the history of the world without violating the rights of our students to their constitutional freedom of religion and their legal freedom from religion while a captive audience in the public school classroom.

There are several reasons why world religions is fundamental content in a book about social studies content. One, social studies standards refer to world religions in the higher elementary grades (fifth and sixth) and the middle school grades (sixth, seventh, eighth). In the absence of curricular attention to world religions in earlier grades, there is little or no prior knowledge on which to address the standards in the upper elementary and middle school grades.

Two, world religions may be considered a cultural marker, if not a primary cultural marker, for the human species. And three, nearly 10 percent of the ideas that changed the world, according to one source, rest in religion (Fernandez-Armesto 2003). Furthermore, just over 10 percent of Hart's 100 most influential persons in history (Hart 1978, 539) are people whose influence is in religion. World religions cannot be ignored merely because we have found it volatile in public education or because many teachers haven't the prior knowledge to teach it properly.

What is "religion"? "Religion conveys the abstract truths of philosophy in the form of images and symbols. Religion, however, is not merely a mythical representation of rational verities; it also takes over where science reaches its limits. No philosophical system can give a rational account of the universe as a whole" (Kraemer 2008, 18).

Religion fills in what science has not completed, at least not enough to satisfy human curiosity. We are pretty sure the universe began, if it began, with an explosion, the effects of which continue (Carroll 2012, 72). We are sure enough to use the "Big Bang" as a scientific beginning. In science, we are rarely more than "pretty sure." We even calculate the magnitude of our sureness with a statistic called "level of confidence." We can be somewhat assured when we have a level of confidence at or beyond around 99 percent. We think we have well-founded confidence that there was something like an explosion.

But we aren't certain what caused it, though we have a good idea. We know if matter is compressed into an infinitely small space, the heat generated in the compression will reach a point at which it will all explode. What we don't know is where all that matter came from that was compressed into an infinitely tiny space.

Human beings aren't very good at not knowing. When we don't know, some of us revert to explanations that do not come from scientific (verifiable and replicable) demonstration. Our explanations are not necessarily untrue just because they may not be verifiable or replicable. They are our best guess, for now.

For example, if we were to look skyward on a clear night, unfettered by ambient light from a population center, we might be able to see what looks like a seemingly insignificant wisp of smoke. It isn't a wisp of smoke, and it isn't insignificant. It is an entire galaxy—the Great Spiral Nebula in Andromeda. It is so far away that the light that strikes our eyes left the surface of Andromeda over 14.5 billion years ago (i.e., 14 and one-half thousand million). It has been traveling at 186,000 miles per second for over 14.5 billion years just to strike our eyes as we gaze skyward. So, the light that strikes our eyes left Andromeda before the Earth began. If we were there instead of here, we could watch the creation of the Earth.

If we could watch, we would have an answer better than "pretty sure." Actually, we are already better than pretty sure about the creation of the earth. What we aren't so sure about is the universe, of which Andromeda represents but an infinitesimal speck. Some people increase their confidence by attributing that first cause to God (a name and a title). Others attribute that first cause to god (an explanation). Still others are satisfied with "pretty sure."

What is religion? It is an explanation that goes beyond the rational account to which Kraemer (2008, 18) referred in his definition. The study of world religions in the elementary and middle school is about rational, scientific (verifiable, reproducible), explanations. Sunday school is about explanations that go beyond the purely rational and scientific. Religion reduces many people's discomfort with not knowing.

There are three bodies of content that fit Monday school in the study of world religions. They are history, geography, and biographical studies. This chapter defines world religions in the context of those three social studies. If our students pose questions that reach beyond the rational and scientific (history, geography, and biography), we tell our students that the questions belong in Sunday school and around the family dinner table.

THE CONTENT FOR TEACHING WORLD RELIGIONS

Merriam-Webster's *Encyclopedia of World Religions* (Doniger 1999) is 1,167 mostly two-columned pages divided into twenty-nine "major articles," eight of which include multiple religious traditions and several others that name single religious traditions (Christianity, for example) with many variations. Parragon Books' *World Religions: Origins, History, Practices, Beliefs, Worldview* (Terhart and Schulze 2007) presents eleven religious traditions, most with profound variations, in 303 heavily illustrated pages. The Teaching Company's *Great World Religions* (2003) contains thirty hours of lectures presented by five professors on five world religions.

Merriam-Websters' *Encyclopedia* names and discusses in detail ten distinct religious traditions: Confucianism, Judaism, Buddhism, Christianity, Hinduism, Islam, Janinism, Shinto, Sikhism, and Taoism. Parragon's *World Religions* names Christianity, Islam, Hinduism, Buddhism, Judaism, Confucianism, Taoism, Shintoism, Mandeanism, and Baha'ism. The Teaching Company's lectures are focused on Hinduism, Islam, Buddhism, Christianity, and Judaism.

There are twelve religious traditions common among the three resources listed here. Of the twelve, four (Buddhism, Christianity, Hinduism, and Islam) appear as major religious traditions in all three sources.

And as is always the case in the social studies, the writers solved the problem of which religious traditions to include in this chapter. By including Judaism with Buddhism, Hinduism, Christianity, and Islam, we offer five religious traditions in this chapter, not because the five represent any sort of "Big Five," but because the five have in common a greater degree of familiarity, thus prior knowledge, however scant, among elementary and middle school students and their teachers than the other hundreds in the resources.

We could be charged with being arbitrary because there are more Sikhs than Jews in the world (23.8 million versus 15.1, respectively), but Sikhs are represented in only one-third of the countries (forty-four) where Judaism is a major religious tradition in 135. Furthermore, there are almost 1 billion nonbelievers in the world. Only Christians, Muslims, and Hindus appear in greater numbers than nonbelievers. But this is a chapter about religious traditions, not nonreligious traditions. So we wrap history, geography, and biography around Christianity, Buddhism, Islam, Judaism, and Hinduism. Readers who want to include other religious traditions, or replace ours with theirs are free to do so. The basic content doesn't change. It is still Monday school, and it still features history, geography, and biography.

HISTORY AND WORLD RELIGIONS

It appears that religion has an anthropological basis in prehistory, long before agriculture (Witherington 2013, 57–60), when people buried their dead in their belief in something like an afterlife. For our purposes, we begin in the dynastic periods of Egypt about 3,000 years before the Christian era (BCE). That is about

5,000 years ago, at about the same time written records began to appear. Religion was polytheistic and zoomorphic.

Hinduism, routinely designated the world's oldest religion, has its beginnings in Indus Valley civilization between 3000 BCE and 1500 BCE. Hinduism began with the invasion of Aryans about 1500 BCE into South Asia (which eventually became known as India) from the lands then known as Persia (Matthews 2010, 67). It was the Aryans (a cultural group in no way associated with twentieth-century usage) who between about 1300 BCE and 1000 BCE composed the Rig-Veda, more than 1,000 hymns that recall the mythology of Hindu gods.

Abraham, his wife Sarah, and their sons Isaac, Jacob, and Ishmael walked the earth between about 1800 and 1600 BCE. Abraham, the patriarch, is the (or *a*) primary prophet for Judaism, Christianity, and Islam. Buddhism appears as the result of the life of Siddhartha Gautama (566–486 BCE). Christianity appeared as a religion in the first century CE, and Islam in 625 CE.

Those are the five, with their historical beginnings: Hinduism (3000–2000 BCE), Judaism, Christianity, and Islam (1800 BCE–625 CE), and Buddhism (566 BCE–486 BCE).

Hinduism

In the 1500s, the Portuguese adopted the word "Hindu" to designate people who lived in the Asian subcontinent region. Before the Portuguese, Arabs in the eleventh century used the word "al-hind" to designate not only the land, but also the people on the land who were not Muslims. Before that, Persians used their term "hindhu," a phonetically changed form of the original Sanskrit "sindhu," which means "river" (Indus). Persians (Muslim) used the term "Hindhu." Arabs used "al-hind," and Europeans (Portuguese) adopted the word "Hindu" in the sixteenth century. The term, therefore, was imposed from the outside and designated a people, not a religious tradition.

Hinduism is a system of multiple religious traditions that originated with the migration (perhaps "invasion") of peoples from Central Asia. The Aryan invaders were warlike and came with horses and chariots, and over time, they settled as farmers. They brought their deities with them and incorporated their own with those of the indigenous peoples they found when they arrived. They built no temples; they had no idols. They worshipped their gods in the open through countless hymns, chants, prayers, and prose. There is no founder, there are no central teachings or codified rites. There is also no single shared belief system or deity. It is both monotheistic and polytheistic. Hinduism is not about this or that, either/or; rather, Hinduism honors possibilities.

But the people of the subcontinent, the people of the river, just like everyone else, seek an explanation. While other religions' explanations tend toward "first cause," Hindus' Sanatana Dharma (Eternal Law, the order that makes life and the larger universe possible) is neither human nor otherwise anthropomorphized. It comprises both being and nonbeing. It is uncreated, eternal, and infinite, a transcendence that merely exists. It is the sole reality, the ultimate cause, foundation, source, and goal of all existence. And it applies to all people for all time.

Sacred texts include the Veda, a collection of scriptures or revelations of Hindu teachings, and the Upanishads, which are considered the earliest source of the Hindu religion. It is the creation of neither human nor god; rather, it is the eternal truth that, in ancient times, was revealed directly to gifted and inspired "seers" who uttered it in Sanskrit, the most perfect language. Hindus recognize one truth. They claim that people around the world merely use different words for it.

The complexity of Hinduism's simplicity makes it, in its way, impossible to capture in a synopsis. Students need to know Hinduism exists. They need to know how it is dramatically different from what they know of the more codified religious traditions, and they need to know that they cannot use what they know of religion as a template to understand Hinduism. Today's Hindu population represents about 13.5 percent of the world's population (www.religioustolerance.org/worldrel.htm).

Buddhism

Approximately 6 percent (385 million) of the world's population identifies with Buddhism. The geographic concentration is largely Japan and Southeast Asia: Nepal, Bhutan, Myanmar, Bangladesh, Thailand, Cambodia, and portions of Southwest China. Many people outside of the population areas probably know Buddhism because of the Dalai Lama, the Tibetan monks, and Buddha statuaries. The name of the Dalai Lama we see in the news is Tenzin Gyatso, the fourteenth Dalai Lama, a lineage that goes back to the thirteenth century.

Siddhartha Gautama lived eighty years, between 566 and 486 BCE. He was born into nobility in what is now Nepal. The basic outlines of his early life are well known. He lived the life of royalty, protected from all bad sights and experiences. Married at sixteen, he was not happy. His wife bore him a son, but his dissatisfaction led him to take a carriage ride outside the palace grounds. There he saw old age, poverty, sickness, and death for the first time, and his driver told him all those were natural. He didn't understand, but he grew to believe that he should live in that world so he could understand. At the age of twenty-nine, he left his house and his family and embarked on his journey to understand, to search for truth. Over the years of his journey, he lived the life of an ascetic. He studied famous masters and in solitude struggled with what it meant to exist as a human being. One day he decided he would sit alone under a fig (bodhi) tree until the truth came to him. It did. It came in the form of the "Four Noble Truths."

The first truth is that life is fundamentally about suffering. The second noble truth means that life is filled with experiences that create desire, and desire becomes death and rebirth. Desire exists because of "I" (ego) that needs to be fed, eternally. Third, when a person comes to a place where I (ego) finally disappears, the desires (the suffering) also disappear. Buddhists understand that this third noble truth may take many lifetimes to achieve. Buddhists believe in transmigration of the soul. And when self has been overcome, the person achieves nirvana or "extinction," as a drop of water that returns to the ocean.

The fourth noble truth is the process of achieving nirvana through the "Eightfold Path"—right views, right thought, right speech, right action, right livelihood, right effort, right mindfulness, and right meditation or concentration. When we think of those, we can see most are not far from what we teach our children about the importance of growing up rather than merely getting older.

The rapid spread of Buddhism two hundred years after the death of Siddhartha Gautama was mostly attributed to the Indian emperor Asoka (272–232 BCE) who adopted Buddhism as his religion, and his influence promoted the spread in India and its neighboring countries, Ceylon (now Sri Lanka) and Burma (now Myanmar), and on to Japan and Korea. Buddhism disappeared in South Asia by the end of the twelfth century but remained influential in Japan, Korea, China, and much of Southeast Asia.

Christianity

The words and countenance of an itinerant Jewish teacher have echoed through the ages with greater power and influence than all the echoes from the greatest among the kings of all Western civilization. Hart (1978) ranks Jesus Christ the third most influential person in history, preceded only by Muhammad and Isaac Newton. His name is Yeshua bin Josef, Joshua son of Joseph. We know him as Jesus of Nazarath, Jesus the Messiah, Jesus the Christ. The religion that carries the designation Jesus the Christ (the Messiah) was not invented, started, nor developed by Jesus. It began after his death, "when the story of Jesus of Nazareth was indeed finished. But, of course, it was really only just beginning" (Hart 2007, 19).

According to New Testament stories, the beginning occurred when women went to the tomb to retrieve Christ's body after the crucifixion, or on the ascension, or with Paul's ministry, depending on what you read and to whom you listen. Most historians mark the location of the early church in Jerusalem primarily under the leadership of Peter. One of its most striking, and significant, attributes was Paul's insistence on inclusiveness, that both Jews and non-Jews could be part of the movement. That is also widely seen as the attribute that could change the world (Hart 2007, 28–29). It is what transformed Christianity from a tribal religion, even a Jewish cult, to a world religion.

Christianity has its scriptural foundations in the Old and New Testaments, the five books of Moses (Torah), and the Christian Bible. Those scriptures were written during a period of approximately 1,300 years in, depending on whom one reads, two, perhaps three, languages.

Christianity started as one church. It was the church of Jesus' god, the church Jesus set upon the rock, as he addressed Peter. It is written that "Peter" meant "rock" (Asimov 1969, 856). Peter later went to Rome and became its first bishop (the bishop of Rome), and because he (Peter) was selected by Jesus himself, he became the father of the church ("papa," a Greek child's reference to "father"), the first in what is taught as a lineage that remains to this day.

However, as was later the case with Islam and conceptions of lineage, not all Christians remained believers in Matthew's perspective (Matthew 16:18). One schism led to the division of the Christian church into Roman Catholic and Eastern Orthodox; another divided the Western Church (Roman Catholic) after the thirteenth-century papal election, from which some Christians decided to follow Urban VI and others Clement VII Martin Luther's 1517 protest against the sales of "indulgences" (grace, or entrance to heaven) led to his "95 Theses," which the evidence suggests he sent to the bishops, and having no reply, he distributed among his friends (Hart 2007, 188). The story of his nailing (most likely tacking) the papers to the church door is also plausible for, at the time, the church door served as the neighborhood bulletin board. The term "protestant" came not from Martin Luther but from those who insisted that their allegiance belonged to their God and not to any emperor.

The Protestant Reformation opened the door to many perspectives on Christianity as the result of diverse readings of scripture, the influence of adherents' diverse opinions regarding original intent, the divine rights of kings, the emergence of Deism, the Enlightenment, and the contests over religious and scientific conceptions of reality. Today, people who identify themselves as Christians represent one-third of the world's population (Time 2009, 568–69).

Judaism

Judaism's beginnings reach back in time as far as 3,800 years. Its father, or founder, is Abraham (Ibrahim in Arabic) (born Abram), whose life began between 1900 and 1800 BCE, depending on whom one reads. Armstrong (2009, 31) dates Yahweh's (God's) call to Abraham to settle in Canaan at 1850 BCE. Gafni (2003) dates the Patriarchs (Abraham, Isaac, and Jacob) between 1800 and 1600 BCE. The second millennium is as close to dating Abraham's life as the *Encyclopedia of World Religions* (Doniger 1999, 6) and Matthews (2010, 240) posit. We use 1800 BCE to accommodate Armstrong's date of 1850 BCE as the date when Abraham was called to inhabit Canaan.

Judaism is a small religion in numbers (0.2 percent of the world's population) with an enormous historical footprint. Moses is a major figure in one portion of Egyptian history. He brings the Ten Commandments to the people of Israel (approximately 1250 BCE). Those people (Israelites and Jews) have suffered expulsion from Spain, isolation in Russia, stereotyping (Martin Luther's 1543 pamphlet entitled Jews and their Lies), and pograms and extermination (Goldstein 2012). After centuries of being driven out of countries and regions, they find their way to their promised land. Judaism is included in this small representation of world religions, not because of its size but because of its influence over nearly 4,000 years of history.

The term "Judaism" appears initially in the Second Book of Maccabees (2:21), which is not in the five books of Hebrew scripture, "those that behaved themselves manfully to their honour for Judaism," in about 124 BCE. It is an ethnic, cultural, political, and geographic designation (people of Judaea, the Judaeans). Certainly, Jewish people identify with ideas about faith and certain practices, but to label Judaism as a religion alone is a constriction. Judaism is a way of life, of thinking and feeling, an identification with homeland that predated the monarchy of King David 1,000 years before the Christian era.

It is a religion of principles and calendar. With regard to the former, from his analysis of the first systematic compendium of Jewish law (Mishnah), Maimonides developed thirteen principles that defined the true meaning of a Jewish way of life (Kraemer 2008, 179–81). The thirteen principles spell out matters of a single unity (creator) that is not subject to physical experience and exists as first cause. The creator is worthy of worship and influences those who possess the greatest natural attributes of perfection (prophets). The creator revealed directly to Moses (not in language as we know it), who was thus guided in composing the Torah (first five books of the Old Testament). Moses was assured that no further law would appear, that all of people's actions are known and rewarded or punished, that there will come a Messiah, and resurrection is attainable.

Judaism's calendar is the factor that unifies the various perspectives within Judaism. The "domains" or groupings of observances in the calendar are High Holy Days, seasonal holidays, festivals, and those most difficult days in Jewish history. Fundamental calendar observances include names most people recognize, for example, Rosh-ha-Shana, Yom Kippur, Passover, Pentecost, and Hanukkah. The latter (Hanukkah), a December recognition of cultural differences between

Judaism and the Greek Hellenism, is unrelated to Christians' recognition of the birth of their Christ and is not, therefore, akin to a "Jewish Christmas."

Islam

It is not uncommon for people to hear messages from their god. It is widely written that Peter heard from his god, as did Paul, Abraham, Mary, Noah, and Joseph Smith. Sometimes messages come directly from a god. Sometimes they come from a god through an intermediary. A messenger brought communications, instructions to be more precise, from a god to a man named Muhammad (570–632 CE). It happened first in 610 and continued for twenty-two years until his death in 632. He was called to be the last of four great prophets (Moses, Abraham, and Jesus before him). All four great prophets spoke in the language, though not "language" as we know it in linguistic terms, of the same god.

Islam is considered one of the three historical religions. Judaism, Christianity, and Islam all have a similar and strong sense of historical destiny.

Muhammad learned that he, an Arab, is a descendent of one of Abraham's sons, Ishmael, born at Abraham's wife Sarah's direction, of Hagar, the Egyptian handmaid of Sarah, because it appeared Sarah could not conceive a child. That would make Muhammad part of the nation of Israel. He also learned that Judaism was founded by Abraham and that the Christian view of one god was actually three gods (father, son, and holy spirit) in one. He heard from his god, through the messenger, that he is the final prophet of the god worshipped by Jews and Christians. And he was instructed to go out and recite.

However, he knew himself as a simple camel driver, though an entrepreneurial camel driver, engaged with his wife Khadijah in transporting goods on the trading market. When he was instructed to go out and recite, he felt he had no tools and no reputation that would make people listen. But the message was clear and non-negotiable, and as he listened more, he understood. He also remembered, for he recited what he heard, and he wrote it down. The message became the holy book of Islam, the Quran, written as poetry in his Arabic language (Matthews 2010, 336). The holy book today is best understood when recited in Arabic.

The term "Islam" means absolute subjugation to the will of God. The religion's Five Pillars exemplify that subjugation. Muslims witness that there is one true god and Muhammad is that god's prophet. They pray five times every day. They tithe to the needy. They fast during the daylight hours of the month of Ramadan, and they make a pilgrimage to Mecca at least once in their lifetimes.

At 21.2 percent of the world's population, Islam is the second most populous and fastest growing religion in the world. The majority of Muslims are Asian and

African, while 20 percent of the world's Muslims are Arab (Esposito 2003, 3). The most populous Muslim nation is Indonesia.

The law is very important in Islam. Known as Shari'ah, it outlines duties Muslims' god places on the community. There are four different forms of Shari'ah law that range from the liberal to the conservative, from use of personal opinion to rejection of personal opinion.

Finally, military matters also characterize the history of Islam. Muhammad is named the most influential person in history (Hart 1987, 33) for his role as prophet in a religion that in one generation spread from the Arabian Peninsula eastward to India and westward as far as France and Spain, along the way including North Africa. Muhammad was a military man of significant leadership skill. The phenomenal speed with which Islam spread was not merely its appeal; it was also an artifact of Muhammad's (and his immediate successors') ability to unify, for the first time, all of Persia, the Byzantium, Spain, Egypt, and Arabia.

GEOGRAPHY AND WORLD RELIGIONS

Half or more of the population of India and Reunion (east of Madagascar, Indian Ocean) is Hindu. Up to 4 percent of populations in South Africa and the United States is Hindu, and as many as 25 percent of the population of Oman (southeast edge of Saudi Arabia) is Hindu. The rest of the world's population is less than 1 percent Hindu.

Both Hinduism and Buddhism give us an opportunity to study the Asian subcontinent. It is a land of dramatic contrasts. To the north and west is the Thar Desert, about the size of South Dakota (77,117 square miles) or Nebraska (77,353 square miles). The Thar Desert is relatively small when compared with Africa's Sahara (3,320,000 square miles), Asia's Gobi (500,000 square miles), and Arabian (900,000 square miles), and the desert in western and southern Australia (250,000 square miles).

From desert land, India shares borders with China and Nepal, where the great Himalaya Mountains reign, with heights from 27,766 feet to 29,035 feet. For perspective, Mount McKinley in Alaska is 20,320 feet high, and the highest peak in Europe (Alps) is at 14,900 feet.

The Indian Ocean borders India on the south; Pakistan to the west; China, Nepal, and Bhutan north and east; and Bangladesh and Myanmar to the west. Pakistan was part of India until the middle of the twentieth century when it broke away, mainly to have a Muslim homeland.

It is also an area of the world where eagles fly and prey on fish from lakes and streams. There are monkeys, lions, tigers, wild boar, a large variety of ungulates (hoofed mammals), and the Sumatran rhinoceros, among many other species, in over a dozen reserves and sanctuaries. And, of course, there are Indian elephants.

Geography includes the study of populations and population changes. There are about 1,298,660,000 people in India. That is nearly 1.3 billion people. There are 300,000,000 people in the United States, or just under one-third the population of India. Of India's 1.3 billion people, 72 percent (935,000,000) are Hindu, 12.3 percent (155,000,000) are Muslim, 6.8 percent (882,000) are Christian, and 0.67 percent (87,000) are Buddhists. There are three times as many Hindus in India as there are people in the United States and just over half as many Muslims as there are people in the United States. Immigration has had a hand in increasing those figures, especially with regard to Muslims, over the decades during which figures are available.

Why the emphasis on India? India is where Hinduism and Buddhism began. Not far away, in spatial perspective, is the Arabian Peninsula, what we know today as Saudi Arabia. Today, the greater Arabian Peninsula includes Saudi Arabia, Yemen, Oman, Iraq, Kuwait, Bahrain, Qatar, Jordan, Israel, Lebanon, Syria, Turkey, Armenia, Azerbaijan, Iran, Pakistan, Afghanistan, Turkmenistan, Uzbekistan, Kyrgyzstan, and Tajikistan. It is what Westerners refer to as the Middle East, but from Chinese perspective, it is West Asia. It is the geography of Judaism, Christianity, and Islam.

The origins and influence of the five world religions in this chapter, therefore range east to what is now India, west to what is now Israel, north to Uzbekistan, south to the southern edge of Saudi Arabia, and up the coast of the Red Sea to Israel. After the death of Muhammad, the southern border of the five religions' influence reached northern Africa. We could refer to those dimensions as a geographic *region* that defines the origins of five major world religions.

Think of world religions in geographic terms. There are three continents named here (Africa, Europe, and Australia), three states of the United States (South Dakota, Nebraska, and Alaska), and twenty-six countries.

Saudi Arabia	Yemen	Oman	Iraq	Kuwait	Bahrain
Qatar	Jordan	Israel	Lebanon		Syria
Turkey	Armenia	Azerbaijan	Iran		Pakistan
Afghanistan	Turkmenistan	Uzbekistan	Kyrgyzstan		Tajikistan
China	Nepal	Myanmar	Bhutan		Bangladesh

Also part of locational geography in that pentagon-shaped piece of the world are the Red Sea, the Persian Gulf, the Mediterranean Sea, the Caspian Sea, the Aral Sea, the Black Sea, the Arabian Sea on the north edge of the Indian Ocean, and the Nile River. There are four terms for the nine bodies of water in the previous sentence. What are the distinguishing characteristics of gulf, sea, river, and ocean? And where are Canaan, Judea, Assyria, Mesopotamia, Carthage, Corinth, Babylon, and Persia?

Buddhists' are distributed primary in Nepal, Bhutan, Myanmar, Bangladesh, Thailand, Cambodia, Sri Lanka, Japan, and portions of southwest China. That would be the major Buddhist *region*. The Abrahamic *region* is a five-sided shape that includes the Middle East, and north Africa along the coast of the Mediter-ranean Sea and eight more bodies of water, including the Nile River. It would be possible to draw a major distribution map that shows the borders of the five world religions emphasized in this chapter. It would also be possible to calculate the square miles in that region and compare those with the square miles of, for example, Montana, Alaska, or Texas, and then of Canada or Siberia or Mongolia. Maps are not mere art forms. We can read maps and use maps to conceptualize the world of religions in spatial terms.

BIOGRAPHIES AND WORLD RELIGIONS

Of the five world religions emphasized in this chapter, Hinduism has no biographi-cal origin. Christianity, Islam, and Judaism all begin with Abraham; and Buddhism begins with Siddhartha Gautama. Two people (Abraham and Siddhartha Gautama) are the main biographical studies for four of the world religions in this chapter.

There are scores of biographical subjects associated with the five world reli-gions in this chapter worthy of at least recognition and study. The fundamental biographical studies argument is that our students are just as able to know and understand Siddhartha Gautama as Benjamin Franklin. The time differential is not relevant because third graders do not have a firm grasp of what 230 years means, and that doesn't keep us from teaching Franklin and Washington. We also teach Egyptian pharaohs (Tutankhamun) who predate both Benjamin Franklin and Siddhartha Gautama by thousands of years and lived in cultures even expert anthropologists do not completely know and understand.

Siddhartha Gautama, Maimonides, and Pope Urban II seem hard and distant because they are not part of our students' prior knowledge, nor our own, for that matter. But those three appear in middle school standards, and if there is no atten-tion in the elementary grades, middle school students will have no prior knowl-edge. The absence of prior knowledge is the signal to teach, not to avoid. If we can teach Martin Luther King Jr. to first graders when he has been deceased for more than three decades, what makes Abraham more difficult? It isn't the years. First graders conceptualize thirty years no better than they conceptualize three hundred or three thousand years. It is the biographical subject that matters.

Biography, however, can raise concerns. It is not uncommon to hear critics claim that students come to know more about Sojourner Truth than Thomas Jef-ferson, more Cesar Chavez than George Washington. Whether such charges re-flect curricular truth is not the point here. The point is that biographical selections can have critical consequences. It is important, therefore, in world religions, as in biographical studies in any curricular focus, to be fair, even, and inclusive when teaching biographies. Three days of Muhammad and one of Jesus Christ is likely to be noticed by students' parents.

APPLICATIONS TO THE CLASSROOM

Table 3.2. Sample Lesson Segment, Primary Grades

Objective: First graders will be able to name two founders of the United States and two founders of world religions. The students will be able to make a descriptive statement about at least three of the four.	*Common Core Standards*: Distinguish between books that tell stories and books that give information. Ask and answer questions about details in text.

Background: Many first graders have George Washington and Abraham Lincoln as biographical studies, so the idea of knowing historical figures is part of many students' prior knowledge. This lesson series capitalizes on what the first graders already know.	*Vocabulary*: *Founder*: There are people who have started countries and religions; they are called "Founders."	*Comprehensibility or Accessibility*: None of the first graders will understand 250 years ago any better than they understand 3000 years ago. The lesson will focus on the names of four people and what they did. Timelines and locational geography will come in later grades when students are capable of understanding.

Procedures: Who remembers who George Washington is? Who remembers who Abraham Lincoln is? Yes, they lived long ago, and they are important in the history of our country. Now we are going to learn about some more people who are important in the history of our country and some other people who are important in the history of what many people believe. So we will learn about people in the history of our country and people who are important in the history of religions. The teacher will use read-aloud as the primary source of information about the four biographical studies.	*Review and Assessment*: The objective of this series of lessons is first graders' ability to name two "founders" in the history of the United States and two "founders" in the history of world religions. Formal assessment rests on each first grader's ability to name four names and three one-sentence descriptions.

Table 3.3. Sample Lesson Segment, Intermediate Grades

Objective: Fifth graders will engage in selection, preparation, and timeline-recording of milestones in biography and history associated with world religions. Students will be able to report on, and write about, how historical timelines can be both horizontal and perpendicular.	*Common Core Standards*: Determine two or more main ideas of a text and explain how they are supported by details. Summarize text. Read on-level text with purpose and understanding. Conduct research that uses several sources to build knowledge.

Background: By the fifth grade, students have experience with timelines. On the possibility that some do not, we review with a wall-to-wall classroom timeline that begins at 2000 BCE and continues to 1500 AD. As review, the teacher places several iconic histories on the timeline: ironworking (2000 BCE), Greeks (1200-400 BCE), Rome (753 BCE-200 AD), Germanic invasions (100 BCE – 500 AD…). Or, teachers enter historical events of their choice. It is important that all entries appear below the horizontal (time) line, and preferably on 5 x 8 cards.	*Vocabulary*: *Horizontal*: as in *horizon* or, roughly, left to right or right to left or east and west *Perpendicular*: a straight line that runs up and down or north and south; in the case of this activity, a perpendicular line runs up and down and through a horizontal line *Timeline*: a horizontal line on which is shown progressive history from "earlier" to the left to "later" to the right.	*Comprehensibility and Accessibility*: The graphic (timeline) is a visual, nonreading, representation of historical events. Notations on =the timeline are recorded on 5 x 8 cards, preferably in colors (blue for biography, green for ages or eras, canary for military, and so forth). The color scheme allows struggling students to use colors to read categories. Save one color for entries above the timeline. As students make entries on the timeline, they will work in dyads in which one member can render support to the other.

Procedures: The historical timeline in place, prepared largely by students over a two-week period, the focus changes to world religions, and students record historical, biographical, and geographic entries on the timeline, above the horizontal line, to show what was happening in the world of religions when King John signed the Magna Carta, for example, or when Justinian ruled, when Leonardo da Vinci lived, and when Columbus sailed. Where does Moses appear above the timeline, Muhammad, the Christian Crusades? All entries above the line will represent a kind of perpendicular timeline so students can see world religions in the context of more familiar or traditional world history.	*Review and Assessment*: When the timeline is well along, the teacher, with the timeline in place as reference, students write, and/or talk, their way through a perpendicular representation on the timeline. For example, Muhammad lived and worked within a century of Columbus sailing, da Vinci painting, and Shakespeare writing.

Table 3.4. Sample Lesson Segment, Middle Levels

Objective: Seventh graders will characterize and place in geographic and historical context fifteen people whose names are associated with world religions.	*Common Core Standards*: Conduct short research projects to answer a question. Write exploratory and/or explanatory test.

Background: The names for this week-long lesson, noted in Procedures," are recognizable (as many as 11) and new (likely at least 4). There is, therefore, some prior knowledge on the list. After the first Knowledge Faire, however, the names are all recognizable to everyone.	*Vocabulary*: *Biography*: The story of someone's life written by other people. *Knowledge*: knowing for recognition, but not necessarily for recall	*Comprehensibility and Accessibility*: Students capitalize on each other's knowledge as well as listings on the Internet. In the former case, they need only ask. In the latter, students who cannot read from the screen use the Three Before Me rule, that is, ask three people before asking the teacher. Students are more comfortable asking when it is part of the game.

Procedures: [Abraham, Isaac, Ishmael, Moses, Martin Luther, King David, Maimonides, Jesus, Paul, Muhammad, Matthew, Pope Urban VI, Pope Urban II, Siddhartha Guatama] On Monday, select two names from the list and by Friday morning learn something geographic and historical about your two names to be able to tell at least two facts about each of the two people you selected. Friday's Knowledge Faire is the time for "reports" about the people selected. Listeners are responsible for taking notes from classmates' reports. Any names from the list not selected and reported during Knowledge Faire (Branca and Fearn 1985) are assigned for Knowledge Faire the following week.	*Review and Assessment*: The teacher prepares a matching test, with names on the left and brief geographic or historical phrases to the right. Students match left names with right descriptions (recognition memory). The criterion for satisfaction of the objective is ten out of fifteen, or 65%. This is an important prior knowledge lesson for what is to come.

REFERENCES

Armstrong, Karen. 2009. *The Case for God*. New York: Alfred A. Knopf.

Asimov, Isaac. 1969. *Asimov's Guide to the Bible: A Historical Look at the Old and New Testaments*. New York: Gramercy Books.

Branca, Tracy, and Leif Fearn. 1985. "The Knowledge Faire." *Gifted/Creative/Talented* (March/April): 28–29.

Carroll, Sean. 2012. "Digging Up the Early Universe." *Discover* (October 2012): 72–74.

Collins, Francis S. 2006. *The Language of God: A Scientist Presents Evidence for Belief*. New York: Free Press.

Doniger, Wendy, ed. 1999. *Encyclopedia of World Religions*. Springfield, MA: Merriam-Webster.

Esposito, John L. 2003. "Great World Religions: Islam." Audio Lecture. Chantilly, VA: The Teaching Company.

Fernandez-Armesto, Felipe. 2003. *Ideas That Changed the World*. London: DK Publishing.

Gafni, Isaish M. 2003. "Great World Religions: Judaism." Audio Lecture. Chantilly, VA: The Teaching Company.

Goldstein, Phyllis. 2012. *A Convenient Hatred: The History of Antisemitism*. Brookline, MA: Facing History and Ourselves.

Hart, David B. 2007. *The Story of Christianity*. London: Quercus.

Hart, Michael H. 1978. *The 100: A Ranking of the Most Influential Persons in History*. Secaucus, NJ: Citadel Press.

Kraemer, Joel L. 2008. *Maimonides: The Life and World of One of Civilization's Greatest Minds*. New York: Doubleday.

Matthews, Warren. 2010. *World Religions*, 6th ed. Belmont, CA: Wadsworth.

Terhart, Franjo, and Janina Schulze. 2007. *World Religions: Origins, History, Practices, Beliefs, Worldview*. Bath, UK: Parragon Books.

Time. 2009. *Time Almanac, 2009*. New York: Encyclopedia Britannica.

Witherington III, Ben. 2013. "Religion at the Dawn of Civilization." *Biblical Archaeology Review* 39 (1): 57–60.

The U.S. Constitution

The Nation's Scripture?

The thirteen colonies, after facing a variety of grievances against England, to which the thirteen colonies owed allegiance, declared their independence on July 2, 1776.

Then they fought a war of independence because England was not about to relinquish their colonies just because the colonies decided they wanted to be independent of the mother country. The colonies prevailed, but winning the war did not establish a "United States of America." There were still thirteen colonies (although the word "state" was starting to appear), now independent, not only from England, but from each other. Their Articles of Confederation and Perpetual Union constituted the framework for how the emerging nation would conduct its affairs.

The Articles said the colonies would be unified and called "The United States of America." But each state was to remain sovereign. The Confederation would be a "firm league of friendship" that ensured common defense, security of liberties, and various protections. People would have free access across all states' borders *as though citizens*. Interested readers can access the complete Articles of Confederation by entering that term in any web browser.

It is important to understand that the Articles of Confederation, while specifying unity among the states, and giving the confederation a name, did not bind the states legally or economically. For example, each independent state's legislature could vote to send money to a national treasury, or to refuse. That turned out to be a significant problem as General Washington pleaded with Congress for resources, so significant a problem, in fact, that because the states did not pay the war costs equally, Robert Morris of Philadelphia personally financed much of the war.

By the mid-1780s, it was clear that the Articles were far too weak a document to enforce unity. A nation in the world community could not function effectively if its constituent states were independent. In 1787, therefore, there was convened in Philadelphia a convention, the purpose of which was to reconstitute the Articles of Confederation to make possible a stronger, more efficient national government. Soon after they convened, it became clear that reconstituting the Articles of Confederation merely perpetuated the problem, and the assembled leaders decided to write a constitution. They did, and adopted it in late summer of 1787.

The intent, the function, of that adopted constitution is possibly best contained in a response to a Mrs. Powell, who yelled from the back of the crowd when Benjamin Franklin emerged from the Philadelphia State House in September 1787. She asked Franklin, Philadelphia's most famous citizen, "Dr. Franklin, what kind of government did you give us? A monarchy or a republic?" Franklin responded, "A republic—if you can keep it!" (Humes 1995, 218).

A republic, an organizational system in which the people through their elected representatives have supreme power in a state or nation-state. It is a form of government in which power is held by the people under their own law. The power of government in a republic is limited by the law, for without law, there can be no freedom. And Franklin said it correctly, "if you can keep it." It's yours. You control it. You can keep it, or you can give it away. Ours is a government that functions just about as well as we want it to function, or to use the epigram variously attributed to de Tocqueville, Ramakrishnan, Jefferson, and Ayn Rand, "We get the government we deserve and deserve the government we get." The essential content in any unit of study on government in the United States of America is the people's responsibility for their own government. That is what "republic" means.

What about "democracy"? In a democracy, everyone has the power of the vote, so the majority always prevails. The majority makes law and enforces law. The majority changes law. The majority rules in a democracy. In the United States, however, there was never any intent to make or permit the majority to have all of the power. Our form of government is divided power. Our constitution, as adopted in 1787, divided power between a legislative and an executive branch and gave the power to interpret the Constitution and to resolve conflicts to a judicial branch.

From the beginning, our constitution divided power even further by dictating that the legislative branch (Article I, of three that pertain to the structure of government in the republic) be divided between a chamber with representatives elected on the basis of the population in the state they were to represent, and a chamber with two senators per state, elected by the legislature of the state they were to represent. (In the early twentieth century, the Seventeenth Amendment placed election of senators in the hands of the people they were to represent.) Our Constitution was, and remains, so explicit with regard to the distinction between "republic" and "democracy" that there is not a single reference to "democracy" in the document.

After adoption, there followed two years of clarifying discussion before ratification in 1789. In those two years, the people discussed and argued about matters of large versus limited government power and protection of state and individual sovereignty. It was during those two years that John Jay, Alexander Hamilton, and

James Madison authored letters and essays that appeared in newspapers. Those letters and essays came to be known as the *Federalist Papers.*

When the Framers met again in 1789, there was still insufficient agreement about the limits of centralized control and protection of the least among us from central government's power. The movement led by James Madison to amend the document took hold, and the Constitution was amended ten times, all at once. Those ten amendments dictated explicitly the rights of every person and the protections of every person against intrusion from government.

Known as the Bill of Rights, the first nine specified, and continue to specify, how every person is protected, not only from the power of government, but from the power of the majority. And the last of the ten indicates directly that any power not explicitly reserved for centralized government belongs to the states and the people. Only when controls on central government and the tyranny of the majority were made explicit did the Framers ratify the Constitution of the United States of America and thereby make the Constitution a definition and explanation of who we are as a people and how we shall govern ourselves.

It has been said that never before in recorded history have so many spectacularly able people come together at the same time for the singular purpose of forming a government that would not make them rulers. The Constitution was ratified in 1789 and remains the longest functioning constitution in the world. It has lived through the doubling of United States' territory (the Louisiana Purchase), enlargement of United States' territory by another third during the Polk administration, and a brutal civil war. Its flexibility has promoted seventeen additional amendments that, among other protections, give the franchise to women, former slaves, and teens.

As the foundation document on which its Supreme Court bases interpretations, deliberations, and rulings, the Constitution has desegregated public schools and public accommodations and ensured voting rights. It has survived overreaches of executive power, various factions' attempts to usurp its legal influence, and vilification for being true to its promise.

Those who see so much of our history as morally, politically, and economically sordid, to be fair, must acknowledge that the Constitution has been properly used to right past wrongs, not for those of the past who were wronged, but for those of the future who, because of the Constitution, have the opportunity to overcome the effects of past wrongs. The history is not a record of righteousness, but neither is it a failure. As Churchill remarked about the American constitutional republic, "the worst form of government, except for all those others that have been tried."

This introduction to the chapter on the U.S. Constitution follows immediately the chapter title, the subtitle of which reads, "The Nation's Scripture?" As a sacred text in a religious sense, no, the Constitution is not scripture. As text that describes who a people are and how a people shall conduct themselves, which scripture does, readers will have to decide. There is no text other than the Constitution that defines who we are as citizens of the United States of America and how we bind together as a free people, under law. The integrity of the nation depends on the next generations' explicit understanding of the Constitution's structures, contents, meanings, and implications. That is what students must learn to be effective citizens.

THE CONTENT FOR TEACHING THE U.S. CONSTITUTION

The preamble can be thrilling, but memorizing it, while not without merit, does not leave students with a sense of what is in the Constitution. The Constitution does not tell us that all men are created equal, that voting creates a majority and the majority rules, that we are a democracy, nor that we are free to talk as we wish. The word in the First Amendment is "speech," not talk; *equality* appears in the Declaration of Independence; *democracy* appears in neither the Constitution nor the Declaration of Independence; and nowhere is it written that anyone "rules." Our students need to read the document and study what the words mean.

We also need to have a sense of what the Framers meant by what they thought and wrote. Much of original intent with regard to the Bill of Rights can be gleaned from the *Federalist Papers* (Kramnick 1987). There are other original intent sources (Rakove 1996) often contained in law review articles. An example focuses on the Second Amendment regarding the alleged right to own firearms (Vandercoy 1994, 1007–39). Given that we are not conducting a class on constitutional law in K–8 classrooms, and this book is not the thousand or more pages in length necessary to merely survey the Constitution, we present only several topics that can help K–8 students come to know and understand their Constitution.

What was to become the United States of America began as separate colonies of European nations. When Englishmen and women landed in what would become Massachusetts, their landing site and the land they expanded into was English. It belonged to England. It was an English colony. And there were twelve more, not all settled by Englishmen and women, but all colonies of their European origins. They stayed separate for more than one hundred years, which meant that when people began talking about a unified country made up of the thirteen colonies, the people in those colonies did not agree on a common cause.

However, the people did agree on a document they called the Articles of Confederation and Perpetual Union. They began drafting it in 1776 and adopted it in 1781. The Articles of Confederation established a legal confederation named "The United States of America." But it was a weak document that could not bear up against the needs of a nation-state.

Our Constitution reflects how the Framers attempted to resolve seven problems: factions, representation, power, states' rights, individual freedom, taxation, and military.

Control of Factions

Political factions (groups whose purpose is to defend their own points of view) are inevitable. One person in a room is likely to agree with everything. Put more than one person in a room and there will be disagreement. The Framers recognized the inevitability of disagreements on the basis of which people form groups or factions. There were two ways to eliminate the effects of factions: try to eliminate factions, or try to make everyone think alike. The Framers knew that if they formed a government run by free people, both of those would fail. So they constructed a government designed to control the effects of factions.

They created an executive branch of government (presidency) whose powers could be balanced by a legislative branch (Congress). Then they divided the legislative branch into two competing chambers, a House of Representatives that served people from each state on the basis of each state's population, and a Senate composed of two people from each state elected to the Senate by each state's own legislature (later, the people of the state).

They also created a Supreme Court with justices nominated by the president and confirmed (seated) by votes of the Senate, with terms uninterrupted by elections, and free of both legislative and executive interference. President Theodore Roosevelt's proposed constitutional amendment to give the people of each state the power to review and, if needed, overthrow a decision of the Court that they did not like (Pringle 1956, 391–97), never got sufficient traction to be taken seriously.

The Framers also created provisions for impeachment of the executive and of the justices, where the impeachment process would begin in the House of Representatives, and if the House voted to impeach, the trial would be conducted in the Senate, with the Chief Justice of the Supreme Court presiding.

The Framers established a tangled web of controls on factions. They made sure that neither the executive nor judicial branches could legislate, but bills passed by the divided legislature could be vetoed by the executive. However, with a sufficiently large majority, an executive's veto could be overridden by the legislature.

Representation

If this is to be a *representative* form of government, how to ensure representation is crucial. The people have to have their voice. However, mere voting does not ensure representation, for large states have more people, and thus their votes are more important than states with small populations. The Framers set up a system that gave voice based on state population (House of Representatives) and on state-specific equality (Senate). Thus, New York and Pennsylvania at the time had more representatives in the House of Representatives than Georgia or Maryland because New York and Pennsylvania were more heavily populated than Georgia and Maryland.

But all four states had exactly two representatives in the Senate. And the House of Representatives and the Senate have to agree before a bill could become a law. Neither the House nor the Senate can control the legislative branch, unless they both represent that same faction (often, political party). Even then a bill cannot become a law if the executive vetoes a House and Senate vote. If the executive does veto a legislative bill, the legislature must have a "super" majority (sixty of one hundred senators, for example, rather than fifty-one of one hundred) to override an executive's veto.

Power

Government is about structures for the exercise of power. In the Framers' United States, representatives elected by the people are in charge. In the United States, the people elect their representatives in the executive and legislative branches, and the executive and legislative branches place justices on the Supreme Court. The power is divided.

The executive can commit troops for military action, but only Congress can declare war. The executive is the commander in chief of the armed forces. The legislature can vote to tax the people; the executive cannot. The executive can ask for government spending in a proposed budget, but only the House of Representatives can originate spending bills. Power is divided.

States' Rights

We are the United *States* of America. It was always a union of states. The states did not give up their sovereignty with their agreement to be *united*. In fact, the states fought hard to maintain their sovereignty, and they established the limits of federal power in the Tenth Amendment to which they agreed before they ratified the Constitution. States' rights has been a primary topic from the beginning.

Do some states have the right to maintain a system of slavery? Do some states have the right to decide where a person may sit on a bus and to which school people may send their children? There is no reference in the Constitution as to who may eat at which lunch counter and attend which school. However, the Fourteenth Amendment to the U.S. Constitution states unambiguously that all citizens must be treated and protected equally. President Dwight Eisenhower sent the militia (National Guard) to Little Rock, Arkansas, to protect the rights of nine students who chose to attend Central High School.

There is no intent here to suggest that the existence of the U.S. Constitution precludes contention. The Fourteenth Amendment makes clear that a state may not divide its citizens into those who do and those who do not enjoy equal benefits and protections, but eight decades later, states insisted that they may. Our constitutional republic requires eternal vigilance.

Individual Freedom

The First Amendment to the U.S. Constitution protects a citizen's right to express his ideas and values. The right of people to demonstrate in the streets cannot be deprived, no matter how offensive the demonstration, as long as the demonstration does not provoke unlawful behavior and is not, itself, unlawful.

The Tenth Amendment, referred to earlier with regard to states' rights, includes the term "people." If control over some action is not delegated to the federal government by Articles I–VII, that action is reserved for the states and the people. There is no ambiguity in the Tenth Amendment.

The Constitution makes clear a single distinction: what is and what is not delegated to the federal government. Those are the boundaries. Postal service, for example, is delegated to the federal government (Article I, Section 8); public education is not, for there is no reference to public education in Articles I–VII.

Taxation

Government has no money of its own. Government does not earn money. The money the government has comes primarily from the people. There are import and export taxes, of course, and interest on money lent to foreign governments, but the government's primary source of the money it needs to conduct the nation's business comes from the people. It is called taxation. The Sixteenth Amendment that authorized government to collect taxes on people's incomes was ratified in 1913. Income and sales are the taxes with which most people are familiar.

There are other federal taxes. For example, in the last third of the last century, Indian tribes opened special stores on the edges of their reservations, and in those stores they sold, among other things, tobacco, liquor, and automobile tires. Why those three products? Indian tribes have "separate nation status" in the United States (explained in chapter 8 on native peoples). For our purposes here, separate nation status means that Indian tribes are exempt from the federal excise taxes that add heavily to the cost of tobacco, liquor, and automobile tires.

Taxation is the responsibility of the legislative branch of federal government. Presidents do not increase or decrease taxes. We pay taxes for the services we want government to provide. Most recent federal government expenditures fall into five main categories: medical care (23 percent of federal spending), social security (20 percent), defense (20 percent), "discretionary" obligations (19 percent), mandatory obligations (12 percent), and interest on the federal debt (6 percent). A breakdown of annual federal expenditures can be accessed on any web browser.

It is important to remember that the government the Framers constructed makes possible all of the services in the previous paragraph as well as taxation to pay for it—all through the representatives elected by the people. The people can elect representatives who will work to reduce or increase expenditures for medical care, social security, national defense, and various other categories of expenditure. The people can also work to elect representatives who will increase, or decrease, the taxation needed to pay for what we want.

Military

The Constitution makes possible the necessary infrastructure for the nation's defense, and to pay for it. Ours is a civilian military. Military officials do not run the military. And the military people do not have access to the resources necessary to run their departments. That comes from Congress (Article I).

The U.S. Constitution has prevailed as the nation's written system for conducting government, largely as the Framers constructed it over two centuries ago, with seventeen additional amendments. It has lived through change the Framers could not have imagined. As a living document, it has adjusted to that unimaginable change. What it demands most is a citizenry that knows what is in it and what that means.

WHAT K–8 TEACHERS MUST KNOW AND UNDERSTAND

The Constitution is often referred to as "the law of the land." We must take care with several conceptions, or misconceptions, about the Constitution, including the reference to the law of the land.

One, the U.S. Constitution is not about laws on which the country rests. There are no laws in the Constitution. Teachers and their students need to understand where laws come from and how they are made.

Two, there are no consequences, in the sense we tend to understand consequences under law, in the Constitution. Nowhere does the Constitution say that if the procedures are not followed, "this" will happen. The Court may deliberate on a procedural matter, or a decision by the executive or a legislator, if an action is brought to the Court, but removal is as close as the Constitution comes to a consequence.

Three, the Constitution does not dictate how state governments are to be constructed. Most states' constitutions reflect the structure of the national constitution, but Nebraska has organized its legislature in one body rather than two.

Four, the head of the executive branch of our constitutional republic (president) does not "run" the country. The president is in charge of the executive branch.

Five, "division of power" or "balance of power" is internal control to ensure that no branch of government can be in a position to run the country.

Six, the first ten amendments of the Constitution, the Bill of Rights, are not at all about protection of the rights of the majority of citizens. The rights in the first ten amendments specify how the least among us, the least powerful among us, are protected from, to use Jefferson's term, the "tyranny of the majority."

Seven, the distinction between *adoption* and *ratification* is fundamental to knowing the history of the Constitution as well as the document's philosophical design.

Eight, the structure and intent of Article III ensures that the Supreme Court is independent and does not, therefore, rule with even the slightest regard for the "will of the people." The justices do not represent the people; they represent the Constitution.

Those eight conceptions are important because they clarify how we must think about the Constitution and how that thinking informs *what* we teach and what students learn.

Constitution Simulations

First, simulated deliberations are based on a false proposition. We suggest to our students that they make a classroom constitution that specifies how we are to behave. The students list eight rules, and when the rules are posted on a Constitution Bulletin Board, the students think they have had a constitution experience relevant to what the Framers did. The students have had no such experience. They merely made a list of rules.

Second, if even one of their rules violates what the teacher thinks is appropriate, that rule is eliminated.

At best, a public school classroom is an autocracy, with the teacher in charge. The constitution-writing simulation is counterproductive because students learn from the activity that there is someone else in charge. That leaves students with a false impression of the rights and responsibilities of citizenship.

Third, classroom elections are good and proper, but they have little to do with the voting that places people in positions to decide how the nation will function. The class president, vice president, representatives, and court justices all do what they do under the direction of the teacher, the autocrat who runs the room. It is fun to hold elections, and it is fun to hold office in the room or the school, but students have to understand that what they are doing is fundamentally different from what they will do if they run for office after school.

The fundamental difference rests in the right to be wrong. Student officeholders are not allowed to make mistakes that affect everyone else in the room or the school. There is always someone who protects students from the consequences of their own ignorance. Outside of school politics, citizens' ignorance plays out in real life and affects citizens' well-being. The right to be wrong makes all the difference.

Finally, in school elections, the majority does, in fact, prevail, and those who do not prevail must play by the majority's rules. There is no protection of the minority's ideas or values. Perhaps a principal steps in and requires accommodation of minority views, but even that is autocratic.

We are not saying that school elections are wrong, nor even that teachers ought not conduct constitution simulations in the fifth grade. Rather, we are saying that if elections and constitutions are in the curriculum to prepare students for their responsible place in the adult constitutional republic, we must show students how their experience in school is different from the nonschool world in which they will live as adult citizens.

THE STRUCTURE OF THE U.S. CONSTITUTION: A LEARNING ACTIVITY

This chapter on the U.S. Constitution is about knowing what the Constitution is, knowing what is in the Constitution, and knowing the role of the Constitution in the life of our country and the lives of the people who live here. We have explained some of that in the narrative portion of this chapter.

Before we move into lesson segments that exemplify instruction about the Constitution, we offer the following activity for students in and after about the fourth grade. Teachers in earlier grades, of course, can select portions of this activity. But fourth graders who can read about as well as we expect from fourth graders can participate in some of the activity. We recommend that students work in dyads.

1. A major purpose for a national census is to

    a. distribute tax dollars equitably.
    b. determine each state's representation in the House of Representatives.
    c. determine each state's representation in the Senate.
    d. protect the rights of minority citizens.

2. The Constitution specifies the makeup of the Congress, its rules, eligibility of candidates, how it is to operate, and its powers. In which branch of federal government is Congress described?

    a. Executive
    b. Judicial
    c. Legislative
    d. Cabinet

    Write the number of the article in which the Constitution articulates the formation of a congress, and paraphrase the major concepts in that article.

3. The Constitution specifies the powers, duties, eligibility, and impeachment procedures regarding the president and vice president. In which article of the Constitution do those specifications appear?

   a. Executive
   b. Judicial
   c. Legislative
   d. Cabinet

   Write the number of the article in which the Constitution articulates matters associated with the offices known as president and vice president, and paraphrase major concepts in that article.

4. The Constitution specifies the nature of the federal court system and the meaning of treason. In which article of the Constitution do matters associated with the federal court system appear?

   a. Executive
   b. Judicial
   c. Legislative
   d. Cabinet

   Write the number of the article in which the Constitution articulates matters associated with the federal court system, and paraphrase major concepts in that article.

5. The Constitution dictates how states are formed, how states deal with federal law, how they deal with citizenship, and the guarantees made by the United States with respect to the states. This section of the Constitution would inform relative to which of the following:

   a. Separation of California into two states
   b. Sale of tobacco grown in Mississippi to citizens in Florida
   c. Denial of free expression in Oregon by a citizen in Idaho
   d. Interstate extradition

6. Which article in the Constitution articulates procedures for amending the Constitution?

   How might the Constitution be amended without adherence to the article named above?

7. Write the number of the article in the Constitution that would resolve a conflict between local community law and state law.

   How would such a conflict be resolved?

8. In which article of the Constitution is there direction regarding circumstances under which the Constitution becomes the "supreme law of the land"?

   What is the essential authority for making the Constitution the "supreme law of the land?

9. There have been twenty-seven amendments to the Constitution during its over two hundred years of existence. The first ten amendments were ratified together as part of the deal between federalists and antifederalists to protect citizens against the power of centralized government and the tyranny of the majority. Match the amendment numbers with the paraphrased amendments.

_____	1	a.	rights of the accused
_____	2	b.	unreasonable search and seizure
_____	3	c.	civil law
_____	4	d.	rights not listed
_____	5	e.	powers of the states and the people
_____	6	f.	right to bear arms (or arm bears?)
_____	7	g.	five freedoms
_____	8	h.	bail, fines, cruel and unusual punishment
_____	9	i.	quartering soldiers ("quartering"?)
_____	10	j.	protection of a person accused of a crime

10. The remaining seventeen amendments have been ratified during the remaining decades of the Constitution's existence. Match the amendment numbers with the paraphrased amendments.

_____	11	a.	end of forced servitude
_____	12	b.	voting rights for black Americans
_____	13	c.	citizens' rights
_____	14	d.	income tax
_____	15	e.	repeal of Prohibition
_____	16	f.	voting age at eighteen
_____	17	g.	suits against the states
_____	18	h.	electing the president and vice president
_____	19	i.	election of senators
_____	20	j.	women's right to vote
_____	21	k.	prohibition of intoxicating liquors
_____	22	l.	restrict president's term of office
_____	23	m.	executive and legislative terms of office
_____	24	n.	presidential succession
_____	25	o.	voting in District of Columbia
_____	26	p.	prohibit poll tax
_____	27	q.	remuneration for senators and representatives

APPLICATIONS TO THE CLASSROOM

Table 4.1. Sample Lesson Segment, Primary Grades

Objective: Kindergarten students will be able to respond "Three" when asked how many branches there are in their Constitution, and they will be able to name at least two of the three branches. There is no inference in the objective that kindergarten students will understand the ideas of "branch, executive, legislative, judicial only that they can use the words and respond "Three" when asked how many.	*Common Core Standards*: Identify words and phrases Identify main topics Use words and phrases acquired through being read to.

Background: Kindergarten students are unlikely to have any prior knowledge regarding the United States Constitution. A reasonable starting point is the structure of the document. This lesson requires only the ability to count to three and to remember two of three new words. Those requirements represent the beginning of prior knowledge.	*Vocabulary*: *Constitution*: Shows how our country is organized. Our room is organized; so is our country. *Branch*: Just as a tree has branches, or parts, our Constitution has branches.	*Comprehensibility and Accessibility*: Everyone in the room starts with little or no prior knowledge, so there is no need to accommodate students who have more or less. The range of knowledge regarding the Constitution may be 1-100. Kindergarteners who learn to satisfy the objective are all at one (1). Teachers mediate the information precisely as they mediate any new information – by informing, repeating, and rehearsing, again and again, over protracted time.

Procedure: Show tree with branches. Talk through labels on the branches: big ones, little ones, middle-sized ones. We can call the branches by name. This one is Eric, this one is Amanda… I have another tree trunk here. It is called the Constitution. It is how our country is organized. The Constitution has three branches. We will be learning about the branches in the next two weeks.	*Review and Assessment*: We remember what we have been learning about the last two weeks. It is the way our country is organized. Good, everyone. Yes, it is the Constitution. It has three branches. Yes, that is right. We have law-makers, the president, and judges.

Table 4.2. Sample Lesson Segment, Intermediate Grades

Objective: Third graders will be able to associate branches of government specified by the Constitution with common descriptions (Executive is president and vice-president; Legislative is Congress which is made up of the House of Representatives and the Senate; and Judicial, which means courts).	*Common Core Standards*: Determine the meanings of words and phrases as they are used in a text. Answer questions to demonstrate understanding of meanings in text. Recall information from print or other sources and sort information into categories.

Background: Third graders will bring as prior knowledge terminology and common phraseology regarding the three branches of government in the Constitution. This lesson builds on that prior knowledge by adding texture to the three common terms and phraseology.	*Vocabulary*: *Executive*: an office that shows a primary leader, not necessarily the one who "runs" things, but one who oversees *Legislature, Congress, House, and Senate*: a branch of government and two houses in that branch where laws are made *Judicial*: a branch of government responsible for making court decisions	*Comprehensibility and Accessibility*: The information in this objective will be delivered mainly by the teacher as oral interactions with students with the aid of charts. There is no reading or writing demanded. In some cases, there may need to be some minor translation into the primary languages spoken by students in the classroom.

Procedure: The teacher names and describes the three branches of government in the Constitution's Articles I, II, and III. These are descriptions as simple as possible while ensuring that students understand the ideas contained in the lesson's objective. The lesson may have to be conducted over several class sessions.	*Review and Assessment*: Students will be able to describe the Constitution's Articles I, II, and III on an age-appropriate level, but clearly distinguishing among the branches with regard to responsibilities.

Table 4.3. Sample Lesson Segment, Middle Levels

Objective: Eighth graders will be able to read and discuss the ten amendments in the Bill of Rights, with specific regard to the words in each amendment and what those words mean.	*Common Core Standards*: Cite the textual evidence that most strongly supports an analysis of what the text says, explicitly, as well as inferentially.

Background: Given prior knowledge from K-7 attention to the Constitution, students have the background to begin explicit and inferential analysis of constitutional word meanings and phraseology.	*Vocabulary*: *Amendment*: to adjust, change, add to *Speech*: distinguish between talk and expression *Militia*: individual, or military organization? *Confront and Cross*: to face and question witnesses	*Comprehensibility and Accessibility*: It is important to help students understand what words and phrases mean, in contexts with which they are familiar. Thus, the distinction in Amendment II, and the phrase in Amendment VI. These meanings have to be mediated by the teacher from sources in both print and technological.

Procedure: The students have a ten-page handout available, one amendment per page, each page divided perpendicularly in half. Dyads read and discuss what the amendment could mean and write their meaning notes on the left half of each page, one amendment per fifteen-minute class session. After each fifteen-minute class session, dyads report aloud what words and phrases were confusing as they talked in dyads. The teacher records those words and phrases on the board, and students record them on the left side of their pages. After passage of a week, the teacher conducts a clarification session on meanings from print and technological sources, or invites a local Bar Association speaker to the classroom to discuss the words and phrases students found confusing. Students record on the right side of their worksheet pages meanings they understand better because of the clarification session(s).	*Review and Assessment*: One week following the clarification session(s), students gather in groups of six and come to general agreement regarding the essential meaning of each of the ten amendments that constitute the Bill of Rights. One week following the groups of six agreements, the students take a written matching test, amendments on the left side and descriptions on the right. Amendments matched incorrectly will be treated in a follow-up clarification session.

REFERENCES

Humes, James C. 1995. *The Wit and Wisdom of Benjamin Franklin*. New York: Gramercy Books.

Kramnick, Isaac, ed. 1987. *James Madison, Alexander Hamilton, and John Jay: The Federalist Papers*. Middlesex, England: Penguin Books.

Pringle, Henry F. 1956. *Theodore Roosevelt*. Old Saybrook, CT: Konecky and Konecky.

Rakove, Jack N. 1996. *Original Meanings: Politics and Ideas in the Making of the Constitution*. New York: Vintage Books.

Vandercoy, David E. 1994. "The History of the Second Amendment." *Valparaiso University Law Review*. Valparaiso University.

CHAPTER 5

The Declaration of Independence

Making the Argument

The Declaration of Independence is an argument. Students must come to understand that there are two kinds of arguments: the argument we *have* and the argument we *make*. The argument we *have* is typically about two or more opinions or perspectives, and those engaged in the argument attempt to marshal their best ideas, evidence, and wit in order to prevail over others in the argument and, therefore, to win. Characteristically, an argument exists in response to a position, a perspective, an idea, or an opinion other than one's own (Andrews 1995).

When we *have* an argument in an informal situation (dinner table, faculty meeting, and so forth) the people involved state their responses to other's opinions, often having formed them even as others were presenting theirs. The result, in informal situations, rarely reaches solutions because people tend to think of their responses while others are presenting theirs, which means no one is listening. If the situation is friendly, it ends with a laugh or two over dessert. Otherwise, it ends with hard feelings, especially if someone in the argument appears to prevail, or win.

The other kind of argument is the one we *make*. It is essentially about one's own opinion or perspective, and the people engaged in the argument attempt to marshal their best ideas, evidence, and wit, but the purpose is not so much to prevail as to inform. In more formal situations, for example, in a debate, two or more sides state their positions or perspectives on a question and then construct their arguments on the basis of their best organization of accumulated evidence and reason. It isn't that participants in debate do not want to prevail, for they certainly do; it is that they know that to prevail, they must make the best argument.

When we *have* arguments, winners are often those with louder voices and more influence, and neither winners nor losers come out better informed. When we *make* arguments, it might be that no one wins, but most everyone comes out better informed. The Declaration of Independence is an argument the Founders *made* to the King of England to inform him that England's colonies in America shall be free, or independent, of England's control.

The Declaration of Independence was drafted by Thomas Jefferson, one among the brightest and most literate of the great minds assembled for the purpose of deliberating about independence. He met with two other intellectual giants (Benjamin Franklin and John Adams) for editorial assistance. The words and phraseology in the document reflect the most literate language of the day, framed especially for international deliberation. While it is not easy reading, it can be read and understood, and the argument cannot be mistaken.

THE CONTENT FOR TEACHING THE DECLARATION OF INDEPENDENCE

In the language of today's writing teachers, the Declaration of Independence is a persuasive essay. It lays out the proposition that the colonies should be and must be independent. It specifies reasons for the proposition—that it is impossible under the circumstances to be separate colonies. It lists eighteen reasons why it is impossible to be colonies beholden to Britain. It summarizes the argument and the intent. Everyone part of the deliberations signed the document.

We refer to the people who deliberated on the Declaration of Independence as "Founders," the "founders" of what was to become the United States of America. They did not establish the United States of America. They established that the colonies would no longer be a part of Great Britain. The result of what they did was not the new nation; it was separation from the former nation. They were colonies of Great Britain for 150 years before 1776. Then they wrote the Declaration of Independence as their formal statement of separation.

At the signing of the Declaration, Alexander Hamilton, upon affixing his signature, said, "We must be unanimous. There must be no pulling different ways; we must all hang together." Benjamin Franklin responded, "We must all hang together, or assuredly we shall all hang separately." An Internet search of "We must all hang together" revealed several variations on Franklin's statement, including "We must all hang together, gentlemen . . . else we shall most assuredly hang separately," and "We must, indeed, all hang together, or most assuredly we shall all hang separately."

The Founders' declaration was an act of treason against the greatest military force on land and sea in the world at the time. The men in the room could have been hanged for treason. Most of them were rich. They had vast holdings of land. Many had large numbers of slaves whom they purchased at considerable cost. They risked everything they had.

And, they were what we call "landed gentry." They were also among the most literate, best educated, and best "connected" people in the world. Adams would represent the new nation in the British king's court when the war was over. Franklin represented the new nation in the French court. Madison framed and wrote the most essential of the civil liberties guaranteed in the Bill of Rights. These were men of extraordinary abilities and international reputation. Had they failed, their family honor would be ruined. They risked, not for their country, because there was no country, but for the principle of independence.

The content we teach when we teach the Declaration of Independence is the history (story grammar), the structure (argument), and the people (biographical studies). There is no reason to avoid teaching students to recite the opener ("When in the course of human events . . .") as an oral language activity and to grapple with the nature and meanings of the language, but we must not confuse students' memorization and recitation abilities with their understanding of the document in historical context.

Irrespective of the grade in which state standards mandate American history, students in any grade can speculate on what the Founders meant by their reference to "all *men* are created equal." Did the Founders mean men as gender, or did they use the term to indicate the generic reference to human beings, as in *mankind* and *the first men to control fire*?

Did they mean to distinguish between light and dark skin and attribute equality to men of light skin? Did they mean that men were *created* equal, but *creation* was long ago, and man's cultural evolution long ago made some men more equal than other men? The discussion is not a debate, and it certainly is not resolved by an in-class vote. Discussion is conducted so students come to understand that the *ideas* in the Declaration of Independence were expressed in language the men at the time understood, but given that language and meanings change over time, what the men meant over two centuries ago may be different now.

Also in the intermediate and middle school grades, students must come to understand that the Declaration of Independence is about *ideas*. There are characters, settings, problems, resolutions, and consequences, but the Declaration, itself, is about ideas. Middle school students should grapple with the ideas. They need to know about David Hume, Cicero, and John Locke. They do not have to be experts in the philosophies, but they cannot understand the Declaration if they do not know the ideas of the people on whose shoulders Jefferson and Adams stood to draft and revise the document.

While studying the opening two paragraphs in the Declaration of Independence, students come upon men having been "endowed by their creator." What did that mean and what does it mean today? What does *endowed* mean, and to what, or to whom, do students think the Founders referred when they used the term *creator*?

In later middle school grades, it could be useful to include the Founders' perspectives on religion. What, for example, does "deism" mean? Who were the Quakers, and what did Quakerism mean? What was Fundamentalism, Puritanism,

Calvinism, agnosticism, atheism, inerrancy? What was the Protestant Reformation, the Great Awakening? The people who wrote and signed the Declaration of Independence used the word *creator*, even as they recognized philosophical foundations from empiricists such as John Locke and David Hume. What did they mean by *creator*? What did they mean by *nature's god*?

None of that would be about anyone's god; rather, it would be discussion of god-concept, if students think the Founders meant the first book of the Bible. Or perhaps students think of a cosmological *creation* (big bang) about which they learned in science class, or a puranic (narratives that describe creation-destruction-creation) conception that creates and destroys over and over again until Brahma's (Hindu) lifespan is completed. Perhaps students think the Founders' reference to *creator* simply meant that man came from somewhere, somehow, so man had to be created. The word occurs in the Declaration; if students are to understand the language in the document, they have to deal with the words and what they may have meant and what they may mean today.

During and after the fourth grade, students should study the eighteen reasons (with nine examples under the thirteenth of the eighteen reasons) why the Founders thought independence had become their only course of action. To understand the example about taxation and representation, students can read how the document captures the problem ("For imposing Taxes on us without our Consent") (capitalized as recorded in the Declaration) and discuss how the reason in the Declaration is expressed in "No taxation without representation." The eighteen reasons (and nine examples), therefore, become part of the content for learning about the Declaration of Independence.

The Declaration of Independence offers a variety of possibilities for instruction. There is the language, the message, the structure, the ideas, the biographies, the geography, and the early history of what was to become the United States of America as well as the history of European colonization in the Americas. There are questions. Who taxed whom and for what reasons? What does taxation mean, and why does it exist? In what forms does taxation occur? What does *landed gentry* mean, *aristocrat*, *property owner*, *common man*, *citizen*, *colonist*, *mankind*, and the other terms in the document? Where is the original Declaration of Independence, and what does it look like?

This chapter can represent a three-to-four-week unit of study that occurs in lesson segments of several days to a week in chunks that occur throughout the year, or in one or two lesson segments that take only one week. The document is represented in the social studies standards of every state. We are responsible for teaching the Declaration of Independence. It is the defining statement of our demand for the freedoms that we specified eleven years later in the two-year process of framing, adopting, and ratifying our Constitution.

STORY GRAMMAR AND THE DECLARATION OF INDEPENDENCE

Declaration, to declare, to announce, to assert, to be sure everyone knows. The Declaration of Independence announced to everyone the intent to do something, and "the powers of the earth" (everyone) needs to know about it. The Declaration honors "a decent respect to the opinions of mankind." The people make their declaration to the powers of the earth and in recognition of the opinions of humankind. To understand the Declaration of Independence is to understand the declaration itself, and to understand the argument.

They declare that they shall "dissolve the political bands which have connected them with another . . . and to assume the separate and equal station to which . . . they are entitled." They declare, therefore, they are *independent*. This people, or unified group of people, declare that they are announcing their independence from another (England), and they are behaving responsibly by making their declaration public.

Students have to understand the purpose of the Declaration of Independence. Teachers have to describe the Declaration in terms that students can understand. The prose is thrilling, but to memorize the first part, while an admirable achievement, provides students with little other than an experience with memorization. There is an idea in the Declaration, and the idea shaped the future of peoples all over the world for the ensuing two centuries. As one immediate example, French reformers realized from America's Declaration and subsequent revolution that reform, even against seemingly impossible odds, is possible. Thirteen years after America's Declaration of Independence, French revolutionaries stormed the Bastille.

To put the Declaration of Independence in terms with which students through the grades can be familiar, we capitalize on the knowledge they have, the knowledge they bring to the task of coming to know and understand the Declaration of Independence. Because the story, the arrangement of characters, setting, problem, and resolution is the first and foremost of children's reading during lap time, they know story grammar. They know what stories are and how they work. They know that stories have one or more characters—a wolf, a pig, a princess, a prince. They know stories occur somewhere—in a castle, on a farm, in a tree house, in Oregon. They know a story is about a problem—how to get across the river, how to tell a parent about something bad, how to teach the wolf pups about the dangers.

They know story problems get solved—the giant falls down from the beanstalk, Cinderella lives happily ever after, the book gets written, they find the treasure. From their earliest memories, children know how stories work. There is a story in the Declaration of Independence.

There are characters. John Adams wrote a previous work that would underpin the Declaration of Independence (Commager and Morris 1967, 56). Adams served on one of two committees (the rights of the colonies) as the member from

Massachusetts. The other committee on which he served was charged with listing the Crown's (England's) infringements.

It was determined by the drafting committee (Roger Sherman, Robert Livingston, Benjamin Franklin, and John Adams) that Thomas Jefferson should draft the Declaration. Jefferson proposed that Adams draft the document, to which Adams said, no, Jefferson should draft, for the reasons that Jefferson was a Virginian and that he (Adams) is obnoxious, suspected, and unpopular, while Jefferson is otherwise; and third because Jefferson can write ten times better than Adams. Jefferson never acknowledged such a conversation. Jefferson said that the committee chose him to draft, so he did (McCullough 2001, 119).

Jefferson worked alone, rapidly, knowing precisely what he was trying to communicate. He didn't have his Virginia library with him in Philadelphia, but he didn't need it. He did not aim for originality or copies from any source. It was to be an expression of the American mind, and because there had never been anything like an American mind before, there was nothing from which to reference.

He borrowed from his own writings on the Virginia constitution and its rights of man. He used George Mason's phrase from the Virginia documents, where the words "all men are born equally free and independent and have certain inherent natural rights" appeared. He considered James Wilson's phraseology from a 1774 pamphlet published in Pennsylvania: "All men are, by nature equal and free: all lawful government is founded on the consent of those who are subject to it."

The foundations were John Locke, David Hume, Francis Hutcheson, Henry St. John Bolingbroke, Daniel Defoe, Cicero. He called upon Adams's "Thoughts on Government": "The purpose of government is the greatest quantity of human happiness" (McCullough 2001, 102).

Back to committee, there were a variety of editions. One changed "truths" as "sacred and undeniable" to "self-evident."

In deliberation of the whole, Richard Henry Lee rose to speak at the State House and said: "That these United Colonies are and of a right ought to be, free and independent states, that they are absolved from all allegiance to the British Crown, and that all political connection between them and the state of Great Britain is, and ought to be, totally dissolved" (McCullough 2001, 118).

John Dickenson, James Wilson, Robert Livingston, and Edward Rutledge spoke in opposition to any declaration of independence until the voice of the people drove them to it. Alexander Hamilton presided throughout the proceedings.

There was a setting. The story of the Declaration of Independence happened somewhere. There was a setting, and it was called Philadelphia. It was June and July. In Philadelphia, Pennsylvania, it was unseasonably mild. (Enter "weather, Philadelphia, July 2, 1776" in a web browser).

The streets were unpaved. Transportation was by horse and carriage. Oxen pulled loaded wagons. The breeze smelled of animal dung. Inside the building where they met, there was no breeze. There were no large windows, no fans, certainly no air-conditioning. The men were dressed in woolen knee britches, waistcoats, and jackets. Light came from candles. Few of the men bathed or cleaned their teeth daily. In their woolen clothing, they perspired freely. It is probable that few of them wore freshly cleaned clothing every day. Their deliberations after dark were lit by candlelight.

There was a problem. Two sides fought it out by mostly respectful debate. One side assumed the position that "the sensible part of the house opposed the motion (to declare). No reason could be assigned for pressing into this measure, but the reason of every madman" (Edward Rutledge in McCullough 2001, 118).

Final vote was delayed for twenty days, until July 1, to allow delegates from the middle states to send for new instructions from their statehouses. In the meantime, the document was drafted.

There was resolution of the problem. At 10:00 a.m. on July 1, 1776, Alexander Hamilton sounded the gavel. The doors closed. Richard Henry Lee's original motion to declare independence was read aloud, again.

Dickenson rose in opposition. It was raining outside when Adams rose in support. He had to make his speech twice, for several delegates arrived after he began.

A preliminary vote that evening had four delegations voting in opposition (Pennsylvania, New York, South Carolina, and Delaware [which demurred because the delegation was not complete]). The first vote was nine to four.

They met again the following morning. A second vote. New York abstained, but Delaware, South Carolina, and Pennsylvania joined the majority. With no vote against, it was done. On July 2, 1776, the American colonies declared their independence.

The document was then worked and reworked again and again. One passage was taken out entirely. In the list of grievances, Jefferson had written: "He (the King) is responsible for the horrors of the slave trade." South Carolina and Georgia objected, and some Northern delegates were uncomfortable with the passage. In fact, slavery, while opposed by many in the North, was nevertheless a social and cultural reality to a greater or lesser extent in all thirteen colonies.

There were consequences. There was a war to be fought, for Great Britain was not about to permit its colonial system, or any part of it, to establish independence. Halfway through the twentieth century Great Britain was still at war holding onto its colonies and protectorates (i.e., India, Egypt, Palestine).

There was the slavery problem that no one wanted to address directly, that everyone knew violated the basic tenets of the documents of freedom that were written, adopted, and ratified during the next three-and-a-half years.

There was the problem of who shall govern. The Adams branch believed that common people should consent, but only the landed intelligentsia should govern. It would be seven executives later (Andrew Jackson) before that attitude was overthrown.

The story ended when the revolution was fought, and independence, declared in the statehouse in Philadelphia and won on the field of battle, was secured. The story of the Constitution follows, but students cannot understand that story until they understand the story of the Declaration. It isn't that the two stories work together, because they do not. It is that the story of the Constitution rests on the story of the Declaration. There is no constitution of the sort the Framers constructed if there is no formal state of independence.

Most solutions and consequences include ambiguities. Keep in mind the ambiguities in this event, particularly with regard to biographical studies. Jefferson drafted the Declaration, with its surpassing language and style about human equality, even as he owned human beings. Adams thought only landed gentry (all male) should have the vote, and he was the lawyer who was so committed to the rights of the accused that he, alone, ensured that the British officers and soldiers who fired in the Boston Massacre had the strongest possible defense in court. And while Andrew Jackson, seventh president, broke the pattern of landed aristocracy controlling the vote, he was also the president responsible for the Indian Removal policy that led to forced marches from tribal lands to what was called "Indian territory," eventually becoming Oklahoma.

Of Jefferson, John F. Kennedy remarked at a gathering of Nobel laureates at a 1962 dinner at the White House, "probably the greatest concentration of talent and genius in this house except for perhaps those times when Thomas Jefferson ate alone." It was John Adams who wrote to his wife Abigail, "It always seemed an iniquitous scheme to me—to fight ourselves for what we are daily robbing and plundering from those who have as good a right to freedom as we have" (McCullough 2001, 104).

It was Andrew Jackson who, unlike Adams who saw slavery as an acid eating through the Union, said that slavery is not the issue at hand, that sectionalism is, that the economy of the South could not survive without slavery, and abolition is what threatened the Union (Brands 2005, 554). As we determine the biographical perspectives we will feature as we teach, in this case the Declaration of Independence, we must take special care to remember that the people about whom we teach were special, by virtue of their place in the founding of the Republic in its formative years, and very complex. Simplistic perspectives on any of them are almost always false.

There has been a good bit of attention in this chapter about reading and understanding the Declaration of Independence in the elementary and middle school grades. The reading is not very complex. Teachers in the elementary grades are all familiar with shared and guided reading. It is not beyond reason for teachers to read aloud, at least, as introduction to the language and ideas of the Declaration, certainly in the third grade, if not before. Remember, it is an introduction to the sounds of the language at first (Fearn 1971); then comes discussion of what the language may have meant and what it may mean today.

ANNOTATING THE DECLARATION OF INDEPENDENCE

Annotation is a way to help students begin to understand what the language can mean. There have been many such annotations to help readers come to understand complex text. Isaac Asimov is known for three such annotations: *Asimov's Guide to the Bible* (1981), *Asimov's Guide to Shakespeare* (2003), and *Asimov's Chronology of the World* (1991).

The following is one of the most widely known annotations of text, in this case the Pledge of Allegiance. Red Skelton is the narrator. He was a comedian, a clown, a commentator, a twentieth-century television icon. Everyone in the middle of the twentieth century knew Red Skelton. On his show one evening, he stood on a bare stage and told a humorous anecdote about his early schooling. Readers can watch the moments of that evening. Enter "Red Skelton, Pledge" on a web browser, go to any of several links, and sit back and listen.

Mr. Skelton quoted his junior high school teacher's observation. "I've been listening to you boys and girls recite the Pledge of Allegiance all semester and it seems as though it is becoming monotonous to you. If I may, may I recite it and try to explain to you the meaning of each word?"

> *I*
> me, an individual, a committee of one.
> *Pledge*
> dedicate all of my worldly goods to give without self pity.
> *Allegiance*
> my love and my devotion.
> *To the flag*
> our standard, Old Glory, a symbol of freedom. Wherever
> she waves, there's respect because your loyalty has given
> her a dignity that shouts freedom is everybody's job!
> *of the United*
> that means that we have all come together.
> *States of America*
> individual communities that have united into forty-eight great states.
> Forty-eight individual communities with pride and dignity and
> purpose; all divided with imaginary boundaries, yet united to
> a common purpose, and that's love for country.

And to the republic
a state in which sovereign power is
invested in representatives chosen by the
people to govern. And government is the people
and it's from the people to the leaders, not from
the leaders to the people.
For which it stands, one nation
one nation under God
meaning "so blessed by God"
Indivisible
incapable of being divided.
With liberty
which is freedom—the right of power to live one's
own life without threats, fear or some sort of retaliation.
And justice
the principle or quality of dealing fairly with others.
For all.

Red Skelton's ending editorial comments aside, he gave heart and breath to the Pledge of Allegiance, recited in classrooms everywhere in a characteristically desultory manner.

The language of the Declaration of Independence feels archaic. Words are not spelled as we think they should be, and capital letters appear sprinkled about without concern for convention. The cursive handwriting has about it a strange look, and the sentences, though clearly in English, do not represent an English that anyone today speaks or writes.

Though not as elegant as Red Skelton's annotation of the Pledge of Allegiance, we offer our annotation of the beginning of the Declaration of Independence as a start for what teachers might use as an object lesson to promote student annotations of other portions of the document.

When in the course
time
as time goes by
of human events,
the times and happenings in which people are involved
it becomes necessary
sometimes we must do something
events make us act
for one people
there are many peoples in the world
and among those many peoples there is
one people, one group of people who find it necessary

to dissolve
to disconnect
to separate
the political bands
the political connections
which have connected them with another,
two peoples, formerly connected,
now are to be separated
and to assume among the powers of the earth,
to be one people that takes on responsibilities
to be responsible as one people
among all the peoples of the earth
the separate and equal station
to be a separate nation equal to all other nations
to no longer be part of another nation
and to be equal to all other nations
to which the laws of nature
free and independent
entitled to the rights of man,
also known as human rights
and of nature's God
the omniscient powers of nature
entitle them,
to have as a right
by virtue of being human
a decent respect
acknowledgment of equality among peoples
and respect for peoples
to the opinions of mankind
what people think and feel
about how the world should be
requires
respect for the opinions of humankind demands
that they should declare
people who decide to be separate and equal
must inform the other peoples of the earth
the causes
what makes one people do what they are about to do
which impel them
they feel they *must* do what they are about to do
to the separation.
the reason for being separate and equal
why they choose to reject the connections and to be separate

APPLICATIONS TO THE CLASSROOM

Table 5.1. Sample Lesson Segment, Primary Grades

Objective: Second graders will associate the names of several Founders with the Declaration of Independence. Second graders will also become familiar with some wording of the Declaration by engaging in the teacher's guidance during the teacher's read-aloud.	*Common Core Standards*: Identify the main topic of selected text as well as the focus (main idea) of selected parts. Describe how reasons support specific points in a textual selection.

Background: Second graders bring prior knowledge about biographical study to the objective. Second graders are also familiar with teacher guidance as text is revealed in teacher read-aloud. While the students are unlikely to know the biographical subjects, they do have the prior knowledge necessary for learn the biographies.	*Vocabulary*: *Human events*: What happens around us as time passes *Necessity*: Requirement, demand *Dissolve:* to end, to change, change from one image or idea to another; sugar dissolves in water	*Comprehensibility and Accessibility*: Biographies are like spelling words; the hard ones are those we don't know. The unknown is equally hard for everyone. To accomplish comprehensibility and accessibility is to make the names and words known. In this lesson segment, all of the students are even.

Procedures: The selected Founders for this lesson segment are Thomas Jefferson, Benjamin Franklin, and John Adams because of their involvement in drafting, revising, and polishing the document. They will be taught about the way we teach George Washington and Abraham Lincoln, both unknown to kindergartners, but introduced for February's Presidents' Month. The teacher reads aloud from age-appropriate biographical selections. Students engage in teacher's guidance, sometimes sentence-by-sentence. Students must come away with an early idea of each biographical figure, for example: Adams the farmer and second president, Jefferson the intellectual and third president, and Franklin the ambassador and inventor. Second graders will also be expected to repeat phrases from the Declaration, based on teacher's oral model (Fearn 1971, 205). The reason for repeats from oral modeling is second graders' direct experience with the language of the Declaration of Independence.	*Review and Assessment*: After a period of time necessary to have listened to and repeated phrases of the Declaration, the teacher reads aloud the whole of the introductory portion of the Declaration, with emphasis on those portions the second graders have studied. There could be some choral reading, but no memorization, in the review. The students will be interviewed by the teacher, individually, with regard to what they know about the three selected Founders.

Table 5.2. Sample Lesson Segment, Intermediate Grades

Objective: Fifth graders will recognize the attributes of argument from their reading, discussion, and dissection of the Declaration of Independence.	*Common Core Standards*: Determine theme… Introduce a topic and state an opinion…create an organizational structure Summarize…

Background: While most fifth graders have been introduced to opinion and persuasion reading and writing, this lesson segment rests on the assumption that they have not. Discussion and dissection of the Declaration is directed at identifying the document's purpose and the argument the Founders made to flesh out the document's purpose. The lesson segment will also clarify (using t-chart) the summarizing protocol regarding main idea and details.	*Vocabulary*: Distinction between *making* an argument and *having* an argument *Introduction* as theme or topic *Rationale* as reasons on which the introduction rests *Summary* as final 2-3 sentences that state main idea and crucial details	*Comprehensibility and Accessibility*: Triads determine the number of reasons in the Declaration's rationale for "…dissolving the political bands which have connected…" The reasons are paragraph-specific, so they are easy to find. Shared reading within each triad ensures that all members of the triad have an opportunity to comprehend each reason.

Procedures: The teacher will clarify the rationale as one of three parts of the Declaration. The teacher will conduct two or more fifteen-minute segments of social studies and/or literacy periods to guided reading of the several reasons for dissolving the bonds between the colonizing nation and the colonies. Fifth graders will meet in triads to talk about how the rationale responds to the opening theme. Each triad is responsible for summarizing the opening theme and the rationale in not fewer than 50 nor more than 70 words.	*Review and Assessment*: The teacher will sponsor informal description and summary sessions in fifth grade and fourth rooms in the school. In each session, four triads will make presentations and respond to questions. The teacher will score each presenting student on a scale of 1 (lo) to 4 (hi) on two criteria: knowledge of the material and voice strength.

Table 5.3. Sample Lesson Segment, Middle Levels

Objective: Eighth graders will describe the essential attributes of the argument in the Declaration of Independence and write a story grammar for two signers they select from lists of four.	*Common Core Standards*: Delineate the argument and specific claims in a text. Write narratives (story) that engage readers in context.

Background: The assumption that eighth graders have read and understand the Declaration as an argument rests on primary and intermediate lesson segments above. If eighth graders have not satisfied the objectives in the two lesson segments above, this lesson segment begins with them.	*Vocabulary*: *Argument*: Describe a perspective, provide one or more reasons on which the perspective rests, and draw a conclusion that follows directly from the reason(s).	Comprehensibility and Accessibility: Students who have satisfied the objectives in he primary and intermediate lesson segments above, and have engaged in story grammar activities in other chapters have the prior knowledge on which comprehensibility in this lesson segment rests.

Procedures: The teacher reviews the nature of argument and how argument is displayed in the Declaration of Independence. In triads, students then discuss argument and the Declaration on and in their own terms. After approximately fifteen minutes of teacher review and student discussion, each student is to write not fewer than 40 nor more than 60 words that describe the Declaration of Independence as an argument. The teacher will review story grammar, provide blank story grammar worksheets, and assign lists of four signers to each student. Students will select two of the signers on their list of four, conduct the necessary research, and pre pare the two story grammars. Lists of four: One list may be John Adams, Samuel Adams, Samuel Chase, Benjamin Rush. Such a list influences eighth graders to write about at least one signer with whom they likely are unfamiliar.	*Review and Assessment*: Students have satisfied the objective when their description of the Declaration of Independence as argument is plausible. Students have satisfied the story grammar portion of the objective when their two story grammars are biographically accurate.

REFERENCES

Andrews, Richard. 1995. *Teaching and Learning Argument*. London: Cassell Wellington House.

Asimov, Isaac. 1981. *Asimov's Guide to the Bible*. New York: Gramercy Books.

———. 1991. *Asimov's Chronology of the World: The History of the World from the Big Bang to Modern Times*. New York: HarperCollins.

———. 2003. *Asimov's Guide to Shakespeare: A Guide to Understanding and Enjoying the Works of Shakespeare*. New York: Avenel.

Brands, H. W. 2005. *Andrew Jackson: The Life and Times*. New York: Random House.

Commager, Henry S., and Richard B. Morris. 1967. *The Spirit of Seventy-Six*. New York: HarperCollins.

Fearn, Leif. 1971. "The Oral Model as a Strategy in Developmental Reading Instruction." *The Reading Teacher* 25(2), 205.

McCullough, David. 2001. *John Adams*. New York: Simon and Schuster.

Personal Finance

Equity and Economic Justice

Personal finance? In grade school? Can we teach personal finance in the first grade, the fourth, even the sixth? What is personal finance? It is the acquisition, management, and enjoyment of money. Personal finance is about money, getting it, managing it, and using it.

Five- to fourteen-year-olds have to learn to ask and understand the answer to the question about how they become one of the people in the United States who understands the system sufficiently well to use it to their benefit. That is the basis for this chapter.

Social studies content includes the field of economics. Upper grade and middle school social studies students learn about the New York Stock Exchange, and many have simulated experiences with the stock market. They may learn about the Federal Reserve, the bond and commodities markets, and the difference between debt and deficit. In the hands of very good teachers with economics backgrounds, students may learn about international preferred currency and why it will take China and India two or more decades to begin to approach first world standards of living.

That is all good, but it is not this chapter's focus. This chapter is about twelve-year-olds beginning to accumulate money so they can live a good life through retirement. The chapter is not about guarantees. It is about increasing the odds. It is not about being rich. It is about having enough. It is about leaving victimhood behind and taking responsibility for one's own equity and economic justice.

THE CONTENT FOR TEACHING PERSONAL FINANCE

When we ask young people what they want to be when they grow up, they never say they want to be poor. Some say they want to be rich, but never poor. Even if what they know best is being poor, they never say they want to remain poor.

Young people know that not being poor means having money, and they understand very early in their lives what money does. They don't call it by a sophisticated name, as B. F. Skinner, the great twentieth-century psychologist, said in an advanced graduate seminar in 1963, "Money doesn't buy everything, but it does provide primary reinforcers of great variety." And they aren't so pithy as Sophie Tucker, the great vaudeville entertainer, who said, "I've been rich and I've been poor, and rich is better." They may not understand the limitations of money, but they understand that having money is better than not having money.

There is nothing political about money. We either have some or we do not, and our politics have nothing to do with it. It isn't geographic. There are people in Rhode Island, in Georgia, in New Mexico, and in Idaho who have some money, and people who do not. Both men and women have money, although some of each gender do not.

Money isn't about ethnicity or nationality. Having or not having money isn't about skin pigmentation or primary language. People of every appearance have enough money while others of the same appearance do not.

People who have more money and people who have less money are different from each other in several important ways.

Many people who have less money experience just as much comfort and security with their money as do people who have more money. Clearly, their similar sense of comfort and security does not come from amounts of money because they have very different amounts. Rather, their sense of comfort and security comes from different ideas about how much money is *enough* to make them feel comfortable and secure. Part of what we teach when we teach personal finance in K–8 classrooms is what *enough* means, and that *enough* means different things to different people.

Many people learn when they are young how important it is to save money. They learn about rainy days and emergencies. They learn about saving for things they want to buy. They learn to put just a little bit of money away each week and to see how much it adds up over time.

Some children learn to take money that adds up over time to a bank where they open an account in their name, deposit their savings each month, and receive a statement from the bank that shows how much money they deposited and how much *interest* the bank paid to use their money. *Interest* is another part of what we teach when we teach personal finance.

Some people learn that saving money, as an end of its own, is a cruel hoax played on people who expect that saving money produces a lot of it. When they realize the hoax, they begin to understand that if they merely save their money, their accumulated money buys less because of *inflation*. We teach *inflation* when we teach personal finance.

People who understand *inflation* do not put their accumulated money in a bank, because they know that the value of their money (what their money can buy) goes down (*inflation*) faster than the bank pays (*interest*) to use the money. Not very many people understand the relationship between *interest* and *inflation*, but those who do tend to have more money than those who do not.

How do some people come to understand *interest* and *inflation*? Most of the people who understand learned at the family dinner table from family members who understand.

Where do people who save, but do not put their accumulated savings in banks, put their money instead? Many people go to a *manager, money manager,* or *financial advisor*. Money managers know how to put money in places where money *works* instead of sitting and losing its value. Those places are Treasury bonds (invest in the federal government), municipal bonds (invest in a town or city), mutual funds (invest in many companies at once), and pieces of separate companies (General Electric, 3M, Microsoft, Intel, and so forth).

People use their accumulated savings to buy small pieces (*shares* or *parts*) of big companies or funds, and *bet* that the companies or funds will get bigger and increase the amount of their money. It is called *investing*. We teach about investing in K–8 classrooms.

Inflation, investing, and interest are taught systematically in expensive private schools where children learn about *how money works* all day and again at the dinner table at home.

It isn't fair that some people have the opportunity to learn how the money system works while others do not. It isn't fair that some people know how to use the money system while others do not.

It also isn't fair to claim that the money system is available to everyone, as though it were air and water. It isn't fair because not everyone knows how to access the money system. It isn't fair if some people can't get it. It is fair only if everyone can get to it. That doesn't mean to have equal money; it means to have the information necessary to participate in the money system.

This chapter is about ensuring that everyone gets information about the money system at school. To use the cliché we hear so often when we talk about making things fair, this chapter is about leveling the playing field where money is the game.

WHAT DO WE TEACH CHILDREN ABOUT PERSONAL FINANCE?

There are five rules for playing the money game and eight personal finance topics students can come to know and understand. Students are in school for thirteen years, fully ten of which are productive years for personal finance instruction.

Rule One: Self-discipline is work.
Rule Two: Opportunity costs (every decision is two decisions).
Rule Three: Money is earned.
Rule Four: Money earns money.
Rule Five: Time is a younger person's friend and an older person's enemy.

Topic 1: How we earn money
Topic 2: The relationship between "seven" and "ten"
Topic 3: *Enough* is a value system
Topic 4: Social Security
Topic 5: Taxation
Topic 6: Gross versus net pay
Topic 7: Inflation
Topic 8: Beating inflation

The following five standards, shown in italics, are largely representative of the kinds of economics standards for many states across the country. Inside the parentheses after each standard are connections to rules and topic numbers listed previously. The alignments here show the extent to which the rules and topics are reflected in the five standards.

1. *Students demonstrate basic economic reasoning skills and an understanding of the economy of the local region.* (Personal finance skills: Rules 1 through 5 and Topics 1 through 8 all apply.)
2. *Describe the ways in which local producers have used and are using natural resources, human resources, and capital resources to produce goods and services in the past and the present.* (That is an economics standard. Personal finance is different from economics.)
3. *Understand that some goods are made locally, somewhere else in the United States, and some abroad.* (That is an economics standard. Personal finance is different from economics.)
4. *Understand that individual economic choices involve trade-offs and the evaluation of benefits and costs.* (Rules 1–4 and Topics 1, 2, and 8 respond to the standard.)
5. *Discuss the relationship of students' "work" in school and their personal human capital.* (Rules 1, 2, and 3 and Topics 3 and 8 respond to the standard.)

Good teachers make connections between what citizens want and what students need. The standards do not routinely reflect the rules and topics for personal finance because the rules and topics satisfy personal finance literacy, while the standards satisfy traditional perspectives on economics.

THE MONEY GAME

The game is played according to rules. People who do not know the rules, or know the rules but do not follow them, or ignore the rules because they believe the system is unfair tend to lose in the game. The rules are not hard, but they do control the money system.

Rule One: The money system is about self-discipline. Nearly everyone can earn money. But to earn money, nearly everyone has to commit the effort. The effort is called work. "Work" does not necessarily mean a formal job, but it does mean effort.

It doesn't seem like work when we get money in greeting cards from parents and relatives. On her birthday, Vanessa received $5.00 from her aunt and uncle, $10.00 from her father and mother, and $7.00 from her grandma. She received $22.00 for her ninth birthday.

Then Vanessa told her mother that she wanted to buy nine songs for her MP3 player for $12.00 and a special hat for $8.00. But her mother reminded Vanessa of the deal they made last year when she received birthday money. The deal was that she would save half of any money she received as a gift.

Vanessa had to save $11.00, and she had to decide what she wouldn't buy with the other $11.00. Deciding is work. She decided to buy the $8.00 hat and only two songs for her MP3 player. Sacrificing seven songs is work. And saving the other $11.00 is work.

Ten-year-old Emilio lives in a twenty-three-condominium complex. He found out that a grocery store wanted someone to hang coupons on condo doorknobs twice each week. He called the number, and a man said Emilio could earn $0.25 for every flier he hung on doorknobs in his condo complex. His mother helped him calculate that he could earn $5.75 for hanging coupon fliers, and if he did it twice each week, he could earn $11.50.

Emilio's mother asked what he would do with all that money. Emilio thought a moment and said he would buy a really good baseball bat and glove. She said that would be okay because he was doing all the work, but she told him that he had to save half of what he earned each week. She said she would be his bank. He had to deposit $5.75 when he was paid. Emilio had to work to earn his money, and he had to work to save half of it.

Rule one is self-discipline, and that means work. If Vanessa and Emilio don't work, they won't accumulate any money. Everything about money starts with self-discipline, and that means work. It is true that some people have to work harder than others to get money. While that does not seem fair, it is real. There is no other way. To decide not to follow the first rule is to decide not to have access to the game. We teach about work in K–8 classrooms.

Rule Two: When we make one decision, we decide not to make another decision. Put another way, when we decide to buy a baseball bat with our money, we also decide not to save that money. It is called *opportunity cost* because the decision to spend instead of save costs the opportunity to be part of the money game. The decision not to play is not necessarily a bad decision, but we have to remember that we had the opportunity to save and decided against it. It is our decision to take advantage or not to take advantage of the opportunity to play the game.

Rule Three: Money is earned. Sometimes, money is a gift, but Emilio earned his money. We could say that Vanessa didn't earn her money, but we have to say that Vanessa's money is just as green as Emilio's money, no matter how she got it. And Vanessa has to work just as hard to save.

Emilio learned that if he were not looking for ways to earn money, he would not have seen the flier from the grocery store. What he learned best was to look for ways to earn money, and that kept him looking.

Soon after her ninth birthday, Vanessa's mother and father told her that they would pay her $3.00 for every A grade she earned on her report card and $2.00 for every B. They also told her she had to save half of what she earned. So if she earned four A grades and one B grade, she would be paid $14.00, and she would save $7.00. They also told her that if she earned four A grades, the value of the grades would increase by $1.00 for the next grading period, so she would earn $4.00 for A grades and $3.00 for B grades.

Rule Four: Money can earn money. After six months, Vanessa had saved $56.00 (her grades plus gifts from her adult relatives), and her mother took her to her investment group of six neighborhood women who pooled their money and invested every six months. Each of the women bought shares for the pool at $50.00 each. Vanessa bought one share for $50.00. When the group met six months later, the treasurer of the group announced that they had averaged 8.5 percent on their investments since the last meeting. Vanessa's investment of $50.00 had earned $4.25.

Emilio had saved $198.00 (his salary plus a bonus he earned for putting the discarded coupons in the trash). His father took him to his bank and showed him how to open a savings account. His father told him to deposit $100.00. Then they went to his father's financial advisor at the same bank. The advisor explained that Emilio could invest his remaining $98.00 in a mutual fund.

Emilio didn't understand what "invest" means, and he didn't understand "mutual fund," either. His father told him he didn't have to understand the terms, but he did have to understand the idea that money can do the work, and the only way to understand that is to do it and watch what happens. Emilio left the bank with $100.00 in his saving account and $98.00 in two mutual funds. A financial report came to him in the mail after six months. The report showed that his savings account now had $98.74 ($0.74 in earned interest at 1.5 percent per year), and his investment account had a balance of $108.50 (dividend of 8.5 percent over the six-month period).

Vanessa and Emilio had a chance to learn the four most important rules in the money game: self-discipline, earning, opportunity cost, and money works. Think of what Vanessa and Emilio will have earned, saved, and invested in one year, two years, and three years if they both exercise self-discipline, a willingness to earn money, and the willingness to invest what they earn.

How Do Children Get Money?

Vanessa and Emilio are lucky. Emilio got a job with the grocery store, and Vanessa's job was to get good grades on her report card. Some other children can get jobs like Vanessa and Emilio did. But usually children have to be more creative about it.

In most communities there are adult service clubs (Lions, Elks, Rotary, Gold Star Mothers, Eastern Star, Boys and Girls Clubs, and so forth). Most of those service clubs have newsletters, and pages in newsletters often have to be collated and stapled. Children can collate and staple paper. Children can pull weeds, cut grass, shovel snow, sweep sidewalks, wash windows, wash cars, run a vacuum cleaner at the neighborhood church, and paint over graffiti at their school.

Children go into business. The old lemonade stand in front of the house is tired, but it used to work. Instead of one child washing cars in the neighborhood, maybe five can get together and form a Saturday car washing business. Everyone learns about recycling in school. If six fifth graders saved aluminum cans in their homes, they might save as much as eight to ten pounds in a month. Scrap aluminum sells for around $0.50 per pound as we write this page.

Children who are ten years old have a lot of stuff from when they were six. Some of that stuff might be sold on eBay or at a family garage sale. If there is a family garage sale, a ten-year-old could sell old books and toys, electronics no longer used, and CDs.

If a nine-, ten-, eleven-, or twelve-year-old is very good at reading, writing, or mathematics, she could earn money by helping six-, seven-, or eight-year-olds with homework after school. Adults in assisted living situations often need someone to read to them. Good readers can earn money by reading to people who can no longer see well enough to read. Every time there is a refund or a rebate, save the money. Look around. Where is there an opportunity just waiting to be filled? There is a surprising amount of money just lying about on the sidewalks.

The key to earning money is to look around for opportunities. Some people work very hard at earning money. Many of those people earn enough money to both save and invest, and if they start early enough, and they use self-discipline, they can accumulate money early in their lives. The earlier they start, the more they have. Here comes another rule.

The Relationship between Seven and Ten

Albert Einstein was asked once what he thought is the most powerful force in the universe. He didn't say it is gravity or electromagnetism or centrifugal force, all such powerful forces that they keep the whole universe working. No, he said the most powerful force in the universe is compound interest.

Compound interest means that the interest earned on money invested becomes part of the money invested, so interest is always figured on a growing total. When Emilio invested his first $100.00, he earned 8.5 percent in six months. He then had $108.50 (8.5 percent interest on $100.00). He was ten years old. If he left his money in the investment account until he turned sixty years of age, and he averaged 7 percent interest on his money, the total in his investment account would be $3,556.67. Why? Because money doubles every ten years at 7 percent interest. At ten years of age, Emilio has five decades before he is sixty, so his $108.50 doubles five times. If he were to earn 10 percent interest on his $108.50 for fifty years, his total would be $15,772.64 because money doubles every seven years at 10 percent interest.

However, there is a caution we all need to know about. Investing money is a gamble. It is possible that the investments will go down, and Emilio, for example, will lose some of his money. It is possible, not probable, but possible. There was a great recession in the United States in 1848, and a stock market crash in 1929, and a recession in 2008 that didn't turn around until 2011. However, the rate of return on invested money over the last one hundred years is positive, not negative. If investors think in the long term, the probability is that they will make money.

When Vanessa turned twenty-one, she graduated from college and became a teacher. She signed a contract for $37,000. If she teaches for thirty years (until she is fifty), her salary will probably average about $60,000. Of her $60,000 salary, she will pay about $18,000 in taxes.

Suppose Vanessa saves and invests only 15 percent of her after-tax salary. That will be about $300 per month. After thirty years of teaching, she could have an investment account of nearly $400,000. Vanessa would not be rich, but she will never be poor. If we understand how the system works, and we use what we understand, money accumulates. But we have to work hard to make the system work in our best interest. The people who do that are usually financially secure. Those who do not are usually not financially secure.

Rule Five: The earlier we begin saving and investing, the more money we will accumulate. That is why we started with Emilio and Vanessa. They are not yet ten years old. If they begin at twenty, they lose the power of one double, and they have to increase the amount they save and invest to get where Emilio and Vanessa are with less money saved and invested each month but with one more double. If they start at forty years of age, they have only two doubles. Time is valuable. Financial security means taking advantage of time.

Enter "compound interest calculator" in your web browser, and put in any figures that seem reasonable. Now, there are two more questions. One, are the figures about Vanessa and Emilio actually true? And two, how much is *enough*? We begin with question one about the accuracy of those figures for Vanessa and Emilio. The answer is no, not without two very important modifications: inflation and taxation.

Inflation

The value of money goes down every year, so what we can buy for $1.00 in one year will cost more the next year. That is called *inflation*. If the annual inflation rate is 2 percent when we put $200.00 in a savings account, exactly one year later the $200.00 will buy $196.00 worth of goods (food, shelter, clothing, tools, entertainment). There will still be $200.00 (plus interest) in the savings account, but it won't buy $200.00 worth of what we want to buy. According to an Internet inflation calculator, in four decades, a $200.00 television set in 1970 would cost $1,110.27 in 2010.

That just doesn't seem fair. We work hard and save our money, earn interest on our savings in a bank, and the value of our money just drips away so after a long time it isn't worth much at all.

What has inflation to do with saving and investing? If all we do is save, we lose a fair amount of the value of the money we save because inflation is greater than the interest we earn on our savings. If we invest at a higher interest rate, we can earn enough in compound interest to at least keep even with an inflation rate of 2 percent to 3 percent, and most likely outrun it if our investments earn more than inflation.

If Vanessa and Emilio earn enough from their invested money to outpace inflation, they can live well. And they probably will, for they each will have a trusted financial advisor whom they pay to move their invested money around to take advantage of the highest possible return.

Taxation

People who live in the United States pay just under 30 percent of our income in taxes, or just about $0.30 of every $1.00. Seven countries have a lower personal tax load (Iceland, Australia, Japan, Ireland, New Zealand, Mexico, and South Korea).

Twenty-two countries in Europe and Asia have an equal to higher personal tax load, from just over 29 percent in Switzerland to 55 percent in Belgium. We pay taxes on just about everything we buy and do.

Who is responsible for the tax load? There is a very good argument that government raises taxes to pay for what the public demands from government. When we stand in the stadium before a ball game, we like watching the wonderfully skilled Navy Leapfrogs drop hundreds of feet onto the fifty-yard line, and we like feeling the stadium tremble when three Navy jets roar over. We like the interstate highway system. We like having potholes filled on our city's streets and the grass kept green in the city park. We want people behind each window at the Department of Motor Vehicles, police officers and firefighters at our door when we need them, and we demand that our national borders are secure. We make demands on government, and our taxes pay for them. Nothing we want is free. The cost of what we want, including government, itself, is enormous.

In the United States, government does not own oil wells, retail stores, or yogurt shops. Government has no money that is not provided by taxpayers.

We all pay income taxes. The Sixteenth Amendment to the U.S. Constitution, which authorized Congress to levy taxes on income, was ratified on March 15, 1913.

Capital gains are what our investments earn. Capital gains tax in 2012 is about 15 percent, but will likely rise to 20 percent or slightly more. So if you sell an investment you have held for a decade, and you sell it for a profit of $50,000 you will likely pay up to 25 percent in capital gains tax.

Property taxes pay for schools, teachers, highway patrol officers, prison guards, and public university professors. There are also federal excise taxes and local and state sales taxes. There are "user fees," like that quarter we put into the slot to keep the lights on for our nighttime tennis game. There is no free lunch. Someone always pays.

When we invest our money, we have to take into account the tax burden. However, there are loopholes in the tax system, available to everyone who knows and uses them. One is called tax sheltering. Enter "tax-sheltering strategies" into a web browser and open the link "What is a tax shelter?" Or, ask a financial advisor.

Our K–8 students have to understand that when they receive a paycheck, the dollars they have to save, invest, and spend are lower than the dollars they earned on the job. They have to understand that there are reasons for the difference between *gross* income and *net* income.

Social Security

Social Security as we know it in the United States started in 1935. Its purpose was to make sure retired people have a modest income on which to live for the rest of their lives. Social Security pays a modest income for however long we live.

Who pays for Social Security? Previous generations of retirees are paid benefits out of contributions of younger workers. Today's workers pay into the system so yesterday's workers can draw benefits. It is called Federal Insurance Contributions Act (FICA). We all see FICA payments in our monthly paychecks. We have to make our fifth, sixth, seventh, and eighth graders aware of Social Security and how, in a very general sense, it works.

Gross versus Net Income

Vanessa signed a teaching contract for $37,000. As soon as she signed her contract, she went to a "gross pay calculator" on her web browser that shows her net or take-home monthly pay at $3,048 ($284.00 deducted each month for federal and state income taxes, Social Security, Medicare, and state disability insurance). When she signs up for medical insurance, her net or take-home pay is reduced by $185.00 (the other half paid by the school district) to $2,898.00. Her financial advisor recommends that she sign up for a tax-sheltered annuity (TSA) to ensure that she saves and invests. She puts $200 in the TSA each month. Her first monthly paycheck is for $2,698.00.

It is important to understand that the salary we earn is not the amount we see on our paycheck. There are at least five deductions that can subtract (deduct) as little as 10 percent of our gross pay and as much as 20 percent. Fifth, sixth, seventh, and eighth graders need to understand that what they earn is not what they get (take home).

What Does Enough Mean?

Yes, of course, it all depends. But that does not mean we cannot calculate a number. Think: food, shelter, clothing, tools, and entertainment. Suppose you (or you and your family) spend $500 per month on food (groceries and eating out), $4,500 on housing, $400 on clothing, $600 on tools (car, mostly), and $600 on entertainment (movies, travel, and so forth). The monthly total is $6,600, or $79,000 per year. If income is $79,000 per year, and expenses are $79,000 per year, it looks like there is *enough*. But there is not *enough* because there has to be monthly saving and investing. If income is $6,600, monthly saving and investing must be $990. Where does the $990 come from each month? Either we earn more money, or we lower expenses. Remember rule one.

It is very important to know how much *enough* is. People who cannot pay for what they need do not have *enough*. People who cannot pay for what they want do not have *enough*. People who can pay for their house, car, and everything else, but do not save and invest do not have *enough*.

People who can pay for what they need and want, but want more, do not have *enough*. Some people seem to be discontented with whatever they have. They will never have *enough*. And some people seem happy with what they have. Those are the people for whom *enough* means being happy with whatever they have.

We all fall into one of those categories. Each of us has to decide what *enough* means. There is no number for everyone, but there is a number for each of us. That is why we need to understand rules one, two, and three.

Rules one, two, and three are content in the personal finance portion of K–8 social studies. Children who learn how to play the game can join the people who have *enough* and, therefore, live secure lives. It is only fair that everyone should know how the game is played, whether or not they decide to play. That is what economic justice and equity mean.

Table 6.1.   Sample Lesson Segment, Primary Grades

Objective: First graders will come to understand that money is earned, and it can be earned in many ways.	*Common Core Standards*: Describe characters in stories and use key details.

Background: First graders can understand the idea of work and having a job to earn money. They bring their own ideas about that to school. This lesson segment focuses on the job as work and work as a way to earn money.	*Vocabulary*: *Work*: In the case of this lesson segment, work is what people do to earn money. *Job:* In the case of this lesson segment, a job is what people have where they work. *Earn*: In this lesson segment, *earn* means to achieve, to get through work.	*Comprehensibility and Accessibility*: As long as this first grade lesson segment stays within the general meanings of the three vocabulary words in the context of the read-aloud and the list of ways to earn money on the board, the ideas can be understood by all of the children.

Procedures: On the first two pages of Tomie de Paola's *Strega Nona's Magic Lessons*, the baker's daughter is working in her father's bakery. Read aloud from those pages and follow with a list on the board of what Bambolona's work entailed. Students respond to the questions, Why do we call it *work*? Does she have a job? What does a job mean? What does a job do? Can children earn money from a job? What kinds of jobs are there? What can people do to earn money?	Review and Assessment: Much of the assessment in this lesson segment is informal, achieved by way of the teacher's observations or monitoring of students' participation. If, because of students' different primary languages, students cannot get the ideas, the teacher must revert back to the procedures and mediate the ideas in a language closer to that with which the children are familiar.

APPLICATIONS TO THE CLASSROOM

Lesson Segment: Intermediate
Lesson Overview: This is an ongoing, financial literacy activity in which third grade students at a triliteracy (English, Spanish, Mandarin) immersion school were exposed to the notion that money can work for them. The students learned to distinguish among various saving options including banks, mutual funds, and stocks. They learned how various interest rates can earn more or less money. Finally, they learned that diversifying their savings is safer and more profitable than investing their money in one place.

Eric is the teacher. He selected five high-achieving and intrinsically motivated students as the money managers. The five students were divided into three groups, each representing a typical financial institution: a bank (one student), a mutual funds group (two students), and a stock investing company (two students). The assigned interest rates were 2 percent for the bank, 5 percent for the mutual funds, and 7 percent for the investment company. All interest rates were based on a two-week time frame. In an effort to incorporate technology into the activity, the teacher asked the three managers to use an Excel spreadsheet to keep track of their "clients'" investments.

The third graders earned points for their work, and they used their points for saving and investing. After two weeks during which the students' points were placed in the three investment options, they were fascinated by their minor revelations.

- "The money invested in the stock company worked harder than the money invested in the bank and mutual funds company."
- "Banks aren't great places to leave your money."
- "Her money earned more because she earned more money in class."

As an extension of the activity, during the next two-week period the teacher created a mini recession to make the mutual fund managers and stockbrokers cut their clients' portfolios by half. The children protested. They didn't like the idea that through no fault of their own, they had lost half their money. They didn't understand this recession and thought it was unfair. They had come to understand how money can earn money, and that this recession took their money away.

Eric explained that sometimes a nation's economy slows down, businesses manufacture fewer products, fewer people are employed because factories make less, and people buy fewer things. When that happens, our investments slow down, as well. The students were eight years old. The personal finance unit was rapidly reaching information overload. They can learn more about recession next year.

They talked about how to mitigate the effects of a recession. The children noticed that while the stockbrokers and mutual fund managers cut their clients' portfolios, the banks remained stable. The children made the following comments:

- "Could I take some of my money from the stock company and put it in the bank?"
- "Do I always have to invest my money in just one place?"
- "The stockbrokers pay more, but they also take away more!"
- "Banks are safer."
- "Why did there have to be a recession?"

The conversation was authentic, the children were engaged, and they asked probing questions. They wanted to know what happened and how to avoid similar outcomes. The teacher introduced the term "diversification." Most of the children chose to put equal amounts of money in each of their three options: bank, mutual funds, and stock market.

After the next two-week cycle, the money managers met with their clients to discuss their portfolios. Before they could hand out earnings, the teacher instructed the managers to collect 15 percent income tax and 15 percent tax on their clients' capital gains. The children protested. But as they discussed the idea of taxes and why we pay them, the children agreed that the roads their parents drive on, the protection provided by law enforcement and fire departments, the uniforms soldiers wear and the planes they fly, and so forth are all valuable services. They didn't like giving up 15 percent of their capital gains and 15 percent of their total income, but they did it because it pays for "things we need."

The third grade unit's purpose was to establish academic vocabulary as prior knowledge for future personal finance units. The third graders got most of the vocabulary quickly. They got "diversification" immediately and used the term (and "diversify") easily when context called for it.

If we taught the content of personal finance in every grade from third to eighth, we would begin to solve the problem of inequity and financial injustice. No one gets equity and justice by waiting for those who have it to give it away.

ADDITIONAL RESOURCE

Bochner, Arthur, and Rose Bochner. 2007. *The Totally Awesome Money Book for Kids.* New York: Free Market Press.

Table 6.2. Sample Lesson Segment, Middle Levels

Objective: Sixth graders will grapple with what *enough* can mean by beginning to understand what life costs.	*Common Core Standards*: Write arguments to support claims with clear reasons and relevant evidence. Write informative/explanatory text to examine a topic and convey ideas, concepts, and information.

Background: Assume this is the first serious focus on the economic meaning of *enough*. Most students in the room will have little or no prior knowledge. Their ideas will be narrow reflections of their 12-year old lives. To move into serious consideration of what *enough* means, students will have to think about matters of income and expenses they have never thought about before.	*Vocabulary*: *Income*: Take-home pay *Expenses*: What it costs to live as we wish to live. *Save and Invest*: What we set aside before we buy clothing, tools, and entertainment *Balance*: An equal relationship between *income* and *expenses*. *Food*: The cost of eating *Shelter*: The cost of housing *Clothing*: The cost of what we wear *Tools*: The cost of transportation and household appliances *Entertainment*: The cost of fun	*Comprehensibility and Accessibility*: These are relative terms in this lesson segment. Some students will understand some ideas immediately, and some of those will understand what the ideas mean in real life, which is six-to-ten years in the future. Some students can begin to understand, and for some students the lesson segment is too early, in some cases, by four-to-six years. We conduct the lesson segment anyway because it will be conducted again in the seventh grade, and the eighth, ninth, and through high school. We never stop helping 6-12 grades understand the economics of their lives.

Procedures: We teach what the vocabulary means, and we offer examples (per month, two people) (salary = $2000; save to invest, $200; food, $200; shelter, $800 [inexpensive apartment]; clothing, $100; tools, $350 [one inexpensive car, with insurance]; entertainment, $100; total = $1750 or $250 left over. We look in the apartment rental and car sales sections of newspapers and the local listings on the Internet to see where we can live, and how, and what we can drive for $800 and $350, respectively. We go to the grocery store and calculate what two people can eat for $200 per month. We calculate how much fun we can have for $100. We start there. We recalculate expenses. We calculate how to increase our monthly earnings. That is how we think about what enough means, for now. The future comes later.	*Review and Assessment*: Sixth graders write a one-page argument, or explanation, about the complexities of what *enough* means. Their writing is scored on a 1-2-3-4 scale, where 1 is low, on three criteria: success at achieving brevity; construction of mission, explanation, and conclusion; and reasonable expectations for sixth-grade mechanical control.

CHAPTER 7

Geography Matters

How We Know Who and Where We Are

"The Mediterranean is the sum of its routes, land routes and sea routes, routes along the rivers and routes along the coasts, an immense network of regular and causal connections, and the life-giving bloodstream of the Mediterranean region" (Kraemer 2008, 6).

Geography is definitions of terms, but if that is all we teach, our students receive little geography. It is also about places and where they are, but if that is all we teach, our students still receive very little geography. Geography in the social studies is about geographic topics, abilities, resources, themes, and standards. Geography is maps and globes, but it is also migration, climate, and why the world gets so much winter wheat from North Dakota, Saskatchewan, and Ukraine.

Geography is about butterflies, wildebeest, and California gray whales. Those creatures all migrate, and geography is about migration. Geography's content is broad. It is the content of geography we teach when we are teaching geography.

THE CONTENT FOR TEACHING GEOGRAPHY

De Blij (2005) wrote about climate change, the rise of China, and global terrorism, all geography topics that geographically literate people have the tools to understand. Geographically nonliterate people believe those topics are political or worse, partisan political.

The tragedy that results from geographic illiteracy is legendary. In modern times, there is Napoleon in Russia, Hitler on the Eastern Front, and certainly the United States versus the Seminole Tribe in Florida. Earlier still is William, the Norman, in the England he thought he had conquered. Far earlier, there are the several kings and other leaders who suffered from their geographic illiteracy at the hands of Alexander the Great, who was geographically literate, which is part of what made him "great."

There are tragedies associated with broken dikes, landslides, and wild fires—most avoidable if we paid attention to the geography. "In the end," Dwight D. Eisenhower remarked, "as is usually the case . . . geography determined the course of events." (Korda 2007, 306). And to make the point one more time, Jean Bodin, sixteenth-century French lawyer and political philosopher, commenting on how to write and comprehend history, wrote, "Begin with geography."

Geography is about places, of course, but it is also about our survival as a species. We fail to teach and learn it at our peril.

Geography is one of those social studies that interacts with, and gives texture to, the other social studies. All of those people we discover in our biographical studies live somewhere, grow up somewhere, do the work that makes them worthy of study somewhere, and die somewhere. Often they do their work somewhere other than where they were born and grew up. And occasionally, geography is associated with what they did that makes them worthy of study.

Part of social studies could be finding out why Marie Curie, who was Polish, did her work in France. Where is Poland? Where is France? We need to put Poland and France onto our mental map of Europe. We also need to understand that, as Alfred Korzybski (general semanticist) remarked about symbols, "The map is not the territory" (Capra 2000).

We will need Poland again when we study Copernicus and Chopin. Think of it! Three people who changed the world through their creative work in physics, astronomy, and music, and they all came from Poland. Is that only locational geography? No. Of the three, who remained essentially Polish? Why did each of the three leave Poland? Did any return? Why do people leave the land of their birth? Locational geography is one of the five geographic themes. "Movement" is another.

The study of movement in geography rests on the basic principle that critters move. Whooping cranes, caribou, whales, wildebeest, and humans all move. Humans started their dramatic move to populate the earth hundreds of thousands of years ago. The evidence shows that a population of approximately 10,000 homo sapiens left what we know today as North Africa and became the human population of the world (Collins 2006, 126; Hawks 2011, 85; Wade 2006, 99). Why did they move, and why them? Why not homo habilis?

Why do California gray whales migrate thousands of miles up the Pacific coast every year? We know those whales have been moving up and down the coast for thousands of years because Indian people we now know as Makah found artifacts in a landslide on the North Pacific coast, among them a vertebra from a California gray whale, embedded with a halibut bone harpoon head dated up to 10,000 years ago. People who visit the Makah museum in Neah Bay can see the artifacts from that landslide. Who are those Makah? Where did they come from? And how did Cherokee from North Carolina and Georgia end up in Oklahoma?

Those are geography questions. But they are history questions, too, and questions that should come up when we teach about Indian people. They are interactions between people and places.

We modify or change the surface of the earth for economic reasons. There is gold (silver, copper, uranium, zinc) in those hills. There is paper in those trees. There are fish in those rivers. That is geography of human adaptation and accommodation, but it is often explained and understood as economics.

Or history. Edward Ball (1998) discovered that he was a mere several generations removed from his ancestors' rice plantations in South Carolina, where his people owned other people known in the family as "the Ball slaves." Where is South Carolina (locational geography), and what is there about South Carolina that makes it rice-growing country (physical geography)? Don't they grow rice under water in Vietnam, Japan, and China (locational and physical geography)? How do we grow rice? What sort of soil is necessary for rice growing? And where? Do they grow rice in Florida?

What does "swamp" mean? What is a desert? How is desert different from swamp if the answer doesn't involve water? What is tundra? What are savanna, taiga, and permafrost? Does climate change over time? How much time? Those are geography questions. The answer, of course, is that climate changes, and it changes for a variety of reasons, one of which is the effects of flora and fauna on the chemistry of the atmosphere. Can chemistry be a geography topic?

In the last 18,000 years, the planet has warmed and cooled dramatically at least six times (de Blij 2005, 76), dramatically enough to have changed the nature of life on earth. Does human existence affect global climate? The answer is yes, of course, because humans modify the environment, and that modification affects atmospheric chemistry (the geography of relationships between humans and places). Of course humans affect global climate.

As mentioned in previous paragraphs, there are five geographic themes: location, place, relations between and among places, movement, and regions. Each of those could be a geography strand in the larger social studies. Each could be a geographic explanation for matters economic or historical. Or each could be a social studies unit.

A sufficiently knowledgeable third, fifth, or seventh grade teacher can use geography as the foundation for standards-specific studies of how humans have affected change in the world. We should at least use geography themes to enhance understanding of read-alouds from *Maniac Magee* (Spinelli 1990), *The Winter Room* (Paulsen 1989), and *Touching Spirit Bear* (Mikaelsen 2001).

Of the three examples of geographic connection above, *Maniac Magee*'s connection is at least about places. The story is set in Pennsylvania. Maniac begins as Jeffrey Lionel Magee in "Bridgeport," on the Susquehanna River. There is a strong flavor of suburban Philadelphia in the book, possibly Norristown, or perhaps Conshohocken, maybe Phoenixville. Valley Forge is in the book, as is Hollidaysburg near the Altoona railroad hub in Central Pennsylvania.

The Susquehanna River is prominent in *Maniac Magee*, and while we are at it, there is the Delaware River in the same general area, and beside the Delaware is the canal by the same name. Pennsylvania is a rectangle, with its little blip at the northwest corner. Bisect north-south and east-west and label the quarters "A" for northwest, "B" for northeast, "C" for southeast, and "D" for southwest. Where are Hollidaysburg, Valley Forge, Philadelphia, Harrisburg, and Pittsburgh? On a wall map or an atlas, can we find New Bloomfield, Harmony, and Kutztown? Where are Maryland, New Jersey, New York, West Virginia, and Ohio? And remember, it was cold for Washington's troops and for Maniac in Pennsylvania's winter.

The Winter Room is set in Minnesota. What about the weather in the book? Gary Paulsen describes the cold. He calls it a *deep cold*, the sort of cold where a farmer can throw a dead sheep on a pile out back of the barn, and it freezes so fast and so thoroughly that it won't smell until late spring, a kind of cold where the ground freezes twelve to fifteen inches down. We run our finger around a globe at the forty-fifth parallel (latitude line) from about the middle of Minnesota east to Mongolia and Kazakhstan and on into Newfoundland to understand the cold in Gary Paulsen's book, to say nothing of what latitude is. The students to whom we read *The Winter Room* have to understand the cold in the book, and the cold is geography.

Touching Spirit Bear is set in Southeast Alaska, Tlingit territory, where people live in direct contact with animals of the forest and coastlines. The geographic focus in *Touching Spirit Bear* is how people live together with the animals, not merely for the purpose of subduing and using the animals around them for domestic work and food.

The five geography themes (location, place, relationships within places, movement, and regions) are roughly parallel to six categories of geography standards. In the following list of six geography standards, examples are shown in italics, by one or more of the five parallel geographic themes in parentheses. This is what we teach if we teach geography.

1. *The World in Spatial Terms:* Mapping information about people, places, and environments. *First graders map their classroom, their school, their bedroom, their house, and the walking route home from school. Second graders learn that the United States map is a rough outline of a parallelogram which, divided into*

four equal quarters, helps second graders visualize and internalize (mental map) the continental map of the United States. (Spatial sense and Location)

2. *Places and Regions:* People's lives are rooted in places we call regions, by which is meant terrain, weather, and population density. The places and regions include geology, hydrology, atmosphere, biology, soils, natural vegetation, architecture, religions, recreation, and transportation.

Second graders learn to name and describe regions other than their own. (Place and Regions) One region with which we are all familiar is the Middle East, or West Asia if you live in China. This is more a region than a collection of countries. For 400 years before World War I, there were conflicts throughout the region, but not over borders (Lewis 2002, 127). Nicolas Pelham, in his introduction to Peter Mansfield's *A History of the Middle East* (1991) emphasizes that fact and its implications for a regional perspective on the Middle East.

3. *Physical Systems:* Interactions between physical attributes of Earth's surface and flora, fauna, and people. *Fifth graders learn about salmon fishing off the Russian peninsula of Kamchatka.* Where, for example, are the rainforests? What are the physical systems, the weather, the terrain, proximity to large bodies of water, the paths of large rivers that make possible the rainforest on the Olympic Peninsula of Washington State? How is that rainforest similar, if at all, and different from, the rainforests along the equator?

What animals do we find in the Olympic Rainforest and the rainforest along the Amazon River, and what kinds of plants grow in the two rainforests? Why are the two rainforests' plants and animals so different when we know both places as rainforests?

How are the Appalachian, Rocky, and Andes mountains alike and different? Where do mountains come from? What does tectonic plate mean? This is all about the study of physical systems, interactions between and among places.

4. *Human Systems:* Distribution, migration, cultures, economic interdependence, settlement, cooperation, and conflict. This means interactions between physical attributes of the planet's surface and the people, flora, and fauna. *Fourth graders learn what immigration means, why people migrate, and the role of immigration in the development of New Mexico, Texas, and big cities in the Northwest.* These are relationships within places. Northwest coastal Indian tribes were, and to a large extent remain, people of the fish, the seal, and the whale. Southeast Texans are people of the fish, especially the shrimp. People and physical systems are interrelated. Geography is the study of those interrelationships.

5. *Environment and Society:* Physical environment is modified by human activities. *Fourth graders learn how farmers in California's Central Valley keep the soil producing, even with several crop cycles each year. Fifth graders study about*

where rice and cotton are grown in the United States, and why. Third graders learn about the environmental effects of the timber and mining industries.

We have a responsibility to protect the vitality and integrity of our environment. This is a geographic, not a political, topic. It also affects the economic environments where people live. Students learn that economic and environmental effects are not zero-sum trade-offs, where we can have one but not the other. We can have the economic pay-offs that we want and the environmental protections we need. But we have to study first, and the study is in the content of geography.

6. *The Uses of Geography:* Interactions between geography and history of the past and history of the future; geography and economics. *Second graders learn the circumstances by which Indian people were moved from their native lands in order to ensure and protect European settlement. Sixth graders study how the Mekong and the Mississippi deltas were formed and how very different people use them in similar ways. Fourth graders, in their study of their home state, learn how geography determined so much of their history.*

Any study of the American Revolution should include the effect of a certain night, and a bluff named Dorchester Heights above Boston, on the British occupation of Boston. How did the "lay" of that land affect the Revolution?

Think of Las Vegas, Nevada, on the edge of Death Valley, dry, barren desert, insufferably hot with no relief in 1945, and in fifteen years it was an entertainment oasis. What does the change tell us about how we need to regard our lifeblood?

Geography Themes

Consider that we don't have mere geography lessons or units; we have geography units and lessons about something. Geography is a tool for understanding things in the contexts of location, place, relationships, movement, and regionality.

The following list offers an opportunity to think *in* geography themes. If you sit down and let your mind wander about for a while, you will come up with your list. Our list is as good a list as anyone else's.

1. A one- to two-week unit on latitude and longitude during which every student has access to a rubber blow-up globe that shows the latitude and longitude grid, continents, oceans, and countries. Students spend several days of ten- to fifteen-minute sessions during which they describe locations around the world. Then we teach the grid, and they use the grid to describe locations.

2. When did humans begin eating potatoes? When did humans discover they can grow potatoes? Where are most potatoes grown in the United States and the world today?

Table 7.1.   Random Generated Themes for Studies in Geography

latitude	longitude	mountains	oceans
lakes	deserts	exports	flora
languages	fauna	history	potatoes
religions	insects	science	anthropology
Marco Polo	equator	honey	wolves
Persia	trout	Waterloo	Mecca
Lake Baikal	coffee	the Vatican	Siam
Genghis Khan	the Kurds	driftwood	exploration
Peach Springs, AZ	Neander River	Talequah, OK	agriculture
Rio Grande River	snow	timber	Prague
gold	Bucks County, PA	population centers	migration

3. Where is Waterloo, Iowa? Why is that town named Waterloo? What is the weather like in Waterloo, in January, April, July, and October? How far from Waterloo is Cedar Falls, Cedar Rapids, and Maquoketa? Use compass points to describe the location of Maquoketa relative to Marshalltown and Dubuque. What are three states that border Iowa? Why is the soil in Iowa black? What do farmers in Iowa grow that appears on road signs with the word "hybrid" on them? What does "hybrid" mean?

Make a list of geography themes for the grade level you teach, or in which you are a practice teacher. With a partner who also has a list, reduce the two lists to a master list of three, and from the three, delete one. In dyads figure a way to combine the two themes into one. Write a social studies unit, around that main theme. Flesh out the unit into not fewer than three lesson segments.

Geography is an enormous field of study. We could wrap the entire social studies curriculum around geography if we decided to and knew enough.

A Change in Perspective: What Do Geographers Do?

Earlier we listed geographic themes and standards. There is another way to think about what we do when we teach geography. This is a perspective with an important history that begins formally in the middle of the last century, in the midst of the Cold War.

One of the more influential studies of curriculum was conducted through a conference at Woods Hole on Cape Cod in 1959 (Bruner 1960). What was so influential about the conference was a change in how curriculum should be viewed. It was a change in perspective. For decades, even centuries, education was the study of what teachers do. After Woods Hole, education became the study of what learners do.

The question that came from Woods Hole is not so much how to teach geography, or any of the other social studies, but what do people who practice geography do when they practice geography? Or put another way, what do geographers do? And in the social studies, what are geographic abilities? Here are twenty geographic activities that feature geographic abilities.

1. Associate geographic aspects (five themes) with current news stories. Students pose all of their current events questions from the five geography themes. Current events becomes geographic, and students experience geography at least once every week.
2. Associate geographic aspects with places in textbooks. The reader response (Rosenblatt 1978) questions we pose as students read from their textbooks (guided reading sessions, for example) are framed geographically. "What did you notice about the geography in the passage? What, if anything, does it remind you of?"
3. Associate geographic aspects with the local community. Students describe their community or neighborhood in geographic terms (immigration, location, weather, terrain, and so forth).
4. Obtain information about places by reading maps. Students use the atlas, which contains various maps (topography, population, demographics, precipitation, and so forth) to respond to questions about agriculture, religious populations, economics, flora, fauna, and more.
5. Determine distance by reading maps. How long, north to south, is Lake Baikal in Siberia? How far is it from Hoquium, Washington, to Lake Quinault in the Olympic Rainforest?
6. Determine compass directions by reading maps. Find the compass rose on a map and describe Poland's location with respect to Belarus, Germany, and Romania.
7. Conduct fieldwork to collect information. Determine settlement areas in a town or city for three different nationalities.
8. Prepare maps for specific purposes. In a science unit about biomes, make a map of the United States that shows at least three biomes.
9. Prepare graphs, charts, tables, or diagrams that display geographic information. Make bar or pie graphs that show exports of foodstuffs from four regions of the United States.

10. Interpret maps to infer information and generalizations. Students study population maps and landform maps, and they draw conclusions about where and why people are more likely to settle in one place than another.

11. Use maps to predict trends. Study population centers on a map of the United States in 1900, 1925, 1950, and 2000. What do the maps suggest about how people move around in the United States?

12. Make a mental map of your state, your nation, your continent, the world. Study maps on which the names of landforms appear, and learn to draw one or more maps that show the landforms.

13. Given a region, determine the pattern, reason, or system of regularity for why people live where they do and generalize that system to other parts of the world. Notice population centers from Minneapolis and St. Paul, Minnesota along the Mississippi River to New Orleans. Study a map of the Danube River in Europe. What do you notice about how the two rivers are similar?

14. Identify and explain "places" in geographic space. "Places" are states and cities, nations, recreational areas, industrial parks, transportation systems, and so forth. Notice how culture and experience influence people's perception of places and regions. What is a good place, and how do people determine goodness? Where are the world religion's holy places, for example?

15. Explain how the physical environment is the essential backbone for all human activity on the earth. Physical environment falls into four categories: atmosphere (climate), surface (plate tectonics, erosion, soil formation), water (oceans, hydrologic cycle), and biology (plants and animals).

16. Identify and explain ecosystems. An ecosystem is a population of plants and animals living and interacting with one another, and with other elements in the physical environment. What are primary geographic aspects that make up ecosystems?

17. Recognize the relationships between human and environmental factors that create economic and cultural systems (settlement, migration, work, and worship). Study immigration patterns in two or more areas of the world.

18. Recognize the relationships between human systems and patterns of conflict and cooperation. Study maps of the Middle East. As a class, describe the ethnic or cultural groups in the Middle East.

19. Recognize how human systems modify the physical environment. Follow the spread of desert lands as a direct consequence of human habitation.

20. Use geographic knowledge to interpret history. What stopped the movement of Germany into Russia in World War II? What kept the United States from prevailing in its "Indian war" with the Seminole Tribe? How did Alexander's geographic knowledge help him to be successful in his military success?

Of the twenty geographic abilities, how many can you accomplish? If you acknowledge to yourself that you can accomplish fewer than half, wouldn't it be a good idea to assume responsibility for learning at least half of the geographic abilities, on your own? If you do not know how to accomplish number eighteen, for example, it is unlikely that you will teach it. If we want our students to be able to accomplish all twenty, and we are unlikely to teach any we cannot accomplish ourselves, there is a conflict.

APPLICATIONS TO THE CLASSROOM

Table 7.2.   Sample Lesson Segment, Primary Grades

Objective: Second graders will use geography themes to inquire about and expand their knowledge about print media stories during current events sessions.	*Common Core Standards*: Ask and answer such questions as who, what, where, when, how to demonstrate understanding of key details in text. (The such as questions are from geographic themes.)

Background: Second graders are familiar with the 5-W questions common in current events presentations. The teacher will make clear that the five geography theme questions are mere variations on the questioning theme.	*Vocabulary*: The teacher will introduce the language of the five geography themes (mapping, regions, living things, populations, and changing the environment). Primarily, the teacher will show second graders how to translate the geographic themes into questions about a current events topic. (See Procedures)	*Comprehensibility and Accessibility*: If second graders can pose 5W questions, they can pose 5-geographic theme questions. The prior knowledge is the same as long as the students know how the themes translate from 5 Ws to 5 geographic themes.

Procedures: The teacher shares a current events piece and asks what questions we ask. The students will volunteer the 5 Ws. The teacher announces there are five different questions, and when we share current events, we select three of the five questions. The teacher will have prepared a chart, to which (s)he refers to teach the vocabulary. For example, the newspaper article is about Elk in the western part of the United States. We study the map <americanprofile.com> (September 30 - October 6, 2012, p. 10) and with the teacher's assistance notice that almost the entire elk population is in the western third of the United States (location). The western third of the country is heavily desert, mountain, and grassland (regions). Most of the Indian people live in the western third of the country (flora, fauna, people). Most immigrants come into the United States across borders in the western United States (populations and migrations). And a significant amount of the mining, damming of rivers, and foresting occurs in the western third of the United States (modification of the physical environment). Many media events can be described geographically as shown in the elk story. Second graders practice geographic inquiry at least once, if not twice each week.	*Review and Assessment*: After several weeks of whole-class geographic descriptions of current events, the teacher divides the class into triads. Each triad receives a newspaper or magazine piece. Each triad's task is to describe the media piece geographically. Then the teacher conducts a geography fair during which second graders present their geographic descriptions of current events. The geography fair each month informs the teacher's subsequent instruction with regard to additional whole-class sessions and students' knowledge of maps and globes

Table 7.3. Sample Lesson Segment, Intermediate Grades

Objective: Fourth graders will become familiar with the locations, populations, and locational origins of Indian tribes in the continental United States. This lesson segment is continuous through the school year.	*Common Core Standards*: Conduct research projects that build knowledge of various aspects of a topic. Integrate visual information with figural information (e.g., maps).

Background: Most fourth graders are familiar with the names of, perhaps, 5-7 Indian tribes, including one or more nearby. Location and migration beyond nearby tribal groups and the names of tribes they know from movies and television, however rarely changes after about the fourth grade. This lesson segment stretches fourth graders' range beyond what they already know.	*Vocabulary*: *Tribe*: A group of Indian people of similar language, location, and culture *Indian*: The generic term of choice for Indian people, originating most likely from an Anglicized version of the Italian in-dios *Native American*: The term used by the U.S. Bureau of the Census to distinguish continental Indian tribes from Hawaiian/Pacific Islanders and native Alaskans	*Comprehensibility and Accessibility*: Fourth graders can generalize a map of the continental United States as a rectangle, with protrusions at the NE, SE, and south central borders, and the SW corner cut off. They can divide the rectangle into four segments: NW, SW, SE, and NE. It is a comprehensible task for fourth graders, in four groups of 7-8, to identify the names of ten tribal groups in their quarter of the United States to include on the chalk map.

Procedures: Fourth graders draw rectangular maps of the continental United States, with irregularities for Maine, Florida, Texas, and Southern California, and with location of the Great Lakes shown. They divide the rectangular map into four largely equal quarters and name states, landforms, and rivers that fit in each quarter. When they become well practiced at the general locational tasks, the teacher introduces the focus of the lesson segment: Indian tribal lands, known mainly as reservations. The teacher locates Makah, for example, in the northwest quarter and Seminole in the southeast quarter, and asks, "Where is Chickasaw?" Using whatever resources are available, students find Indian tribal lands, write the name on a 3x3 sticky, and place it on a 3' by 5' outline map of the United States posted on one wall of the classroom. When ten reservations are shown on the map, the teacher changes the task. "Before you place a tribal name on the map, you have to write the tribe's population, primary language, and one cultural characteristic on the back of the sticky. Begin with the ten already on the map." One ten-minute session per week is allotted for the task.	*Review and Assessment*: The activity described under "procedures" continues through the year and culminates in the students' chalk drawing of the continental United States on a concrete playground, with locations shown of at least sixty tribal groups. Because everyone in the school knows of the project (there is a huge map on the playground), the fourth graders respond to invitations from other classes in the school by teaching other students about Indian tribal names, locations, language(s), and cultural characteristics.

Table 7.4. Sample Lesson Segment, Middle Levels

Objective: Sixth graders will be able to identify Siberia and its borders (Ural Mountains, Kazakhstan, Mongolia, China, and the Arctic and Pacific Oceans). Sixth graders will identify Lake Baikal north of Mongolia between Kazakhstan and China. Sixth graders will be able to identify and write briefly about Lake Baikal as a source of the world's fresh water, an ecosystem, and home of both human and animal life as well as plant life.	*Common Core Standards*: Write exploratory/explanatory texts to examine a topic and convey ideas concepts, and information through selection and organization of relevant content

Background: This is new territory for most sixth graders. They will need maps and globes, certainly, as well as help in pronouncing words they have never seen before in a global area they have rarely thought about. The teacher will capitalize on sixth graders' prior knowledge about maps and globes and bodies of water. Two issues of *National Geographic* (June 1992 and 1998) are specifically useful in this unit of study. In addition, Farley Mowat's *The Siberians* (New York: Bantam, 1970), as read-aloud, will provide human texture for the study.	*Vocabulary*: *Tiaga*: boreal forest or marshy pine *Tundra*: treeless plain, coldest of the biomes *Biome*: area of geographic similarity *Locations:* Siberia, Lake Baikal, Irkutsk, Ural Mountains *People*: Buryat, the largest native group in Siberia, Mongols in heritage	*Comprehensibility and Accessibility*: This is a unit of study for which it is inappropriate to hold sixth graders fully responsible. The unit is far more orientation than mastery. Often working in dyads or triads, sixth graders work on locational geography. Their prior knowledge about biomes will be associated with what is probably a new area of study. Images in *National Geographic*, to which students respond with what they notice and what it reminds them of (reader response prompts) increase familiarity.

Procedures: Students engage in class-wide locational geography searches; teacher read-aloud from *The Siberians*; students review of *National Geographic* in dyads and writing to reader response prompts; and much practice with maps and globes to get a sense of the extreme dimensions, weather, and emptiness associated with Siberia will dominate the unit. The focus on Lake Baikal will include nearby Irkutsk as well as the lake as human treasure and ecological challenges.	*Review and Assessment*: Sixth graders' explanatory writing, with emphasis on brevity (100-150 words) will be assessed against three criteria: content accuracy, achievement of brevity, and sixth-grade-appropriate mechanical control.

REFERENCES

Ball, Edward. 1998. *Slaves in the Family*. New York: Ballantine Publishing.

Bruner, Jerome. 1960. *The Process of Education*. New York: Vintage Books.

Capra, Fritjof. 2000. *The Tao of Physics*. Boston: Shambhala Publications.

Collins, Francis S. 2006. *The Language of God: A Scientist Presents Evidence for Belief*. New York: Free Press.

De Blij, Harm. 2005. *Why Geography Matters*. New York: Oxford University Press.

Hawks, John. 2011. *The Rise of Humans: Great Scientific Debates*. Chantilly, VA: The Teaching Company.

Korda, Michael. 2007. *Ike: An American Hero*. New York: Harper Perennial.

Kramer, Joel L., 2008. *Maimonides: The Life and World of One of Civilizations' Greatest Minds*. New York: Doubleday.

Lewis, Bernard. 2002. *What Went Wrong: Western Impact and Middle Eastern Response*. New York: Oxford University Press.

Mansfield, Peter. 1991. *A History of the Middle East*. 2nd ed. New York: Penguin.

Mikaelsen, B. 2001. *Touching Spirit Bear*. New York: Harper Trophy, 2001.

Mowat, Farley. 1959. *The Desperate People*, Toronto: Seal Books.

Paulsen, Gary. 1989. *The Winter Room*. New York: Bantam Doubleday Dell.

Rosenblatt, L. M. 1978. *The Reader, The Text, The Poem: The Transactional Theory of the Literary Work*. Carbondale: Southern Illinois University Press.

Spinelli, Jerry. 1990. *Maniac Magee*. New York: Little, Brown.

Wade, Nicholas. 2006. *Before the Dawn: Recovering the Lost History of Our Ancestors*. New York: Penguin.

CHAPTER 8

Native Peoples

It's About Now!

Shortly after the publication of his book, *Custer Died for Your Sins*, author Vine Deloria Jr. (1969), Pine Ridge Sioux, was a guest on "The Tonight Show Starring Johnny Carson." Carson opened the conversation with a comment about the history of Indian people and the United States.

Deloria turned to his host and said, "If you want to talk about history, talk to somebody else. I'm here to talk about today, tonight, about a little girl at Standing Rock or Pine Ridge or Rosebud or Cheyenne River or Crow Creek or any of the others, going to sleep tonight [it was January] in the back of an abandon Chevy, covered with a ratty old blanket, and in the morning she'll walk three miles to school, in the snow, wearing low-cut sneakers, a cotton dress, and a basketball warm-up jacket. And it's a lousy school. That's what I'm here to talk about."

The late Vine Deloria is Sioux, or more generically, Lakota, and before that, Dakota. In this chapter, we refer to many tribes of native peoples, *all in the United States*, including Hawaii and Alaska. We acknowledge that there are native peoples in Brazil, Australia, Siberia, Finland, Mongolia, and elsewhere. We limit our attention in this chapter to the United States because elementary school studies of native peoples focus almost exclusively on native peoples in the United States.

Indian people are not museum artifacts or ecological icons. They aren't disadvantaged, culturally or otherwise. And they do not need to be told what they should be called. When Russell Means, Oglala Sioux, was asked which he preferred, "Native American" or "Indian," he replied, "I don't give a *hoot* what you call me. Just get the *heck* out of my way." (He didn't say *hoot* and *heck*, but those terms will have to do here.)

Bob Roessel went to the Navajo Reservation at age twenty-four and, in the words of Joe Shirley, president of the Navajo Nation at Roessel's memorial, "embraced our culture with his whole heart. Our Navajo family has truly lost one of our sons, one of our brothers."

Bob Roessel's speech was direct, staccato, and often loud enough to be heard in the next county, especially when his rage was tripped by a government bureaucrat's failure to regard Indian people properly. At a meeting in the mid-1960s, he cut off a Bureau of Indian Affairs official who said that Navajos might not have the background to make a certain decision safely, slammed his palm on the table and roared, "*Dagnabbit*, Indian people have the right to be wrong!" (Bob Roessel would never use a term like *dagnabbit*, but that will have to do here.)

Indian tribes have formed their own school systems as alternatives to government and church schools. They have sent their sons and daughters to law and medical schools, and Indian engineers work with Indian architects to construct buildings and bridges on and off Indian land.

Indian people are not victims. They do not suffer a special plight. They appreciate the environment, as everyone else does, and they exploit it for the same reasons. They are not culturally monolithic. There is no Indian culture. There is no Indian language.

Indian people live in every state and in every city of significant size. Indian people have names, today and centuries ago. They think and talk, and they did in the fifteenth century, or the tenth, when Europeans arrived in the Americas. They work at the same jobs at which non-Indians work. They are no more arts- and crafts-oriented than anyone else. They go to school, marry, have families, and raise their children to be good citizens.

There are rich tribes and poor tribes, Indian people of great national influence and others of little national influence. No commentary about Indian people applies to all Indian people, any more than does all commentary about any "group" apply to all members of any group.

Indian people are, if we insist on the term, "diverse," not with regard to non-Indians, but among Indian people, themselves. Pueblo people of Picuris and Cochiti are different from one another just as are Apache people of Jicarilla and White Mountain different from one another. Furthermore, the people of the nineteen New Mexico pueblos have many cultural and historical attributes in common that they share with no tribal group that is not Pueblo.

Indian people, like everyone else, keep changing. Anyone who was familiar with the cultural and political workings of any Indian tribal group one decade ago, and hasn't had contact since, and thinks he is still familiar, doesn't know Indian people, and isn't.

This chapter is about what K–8 students need to learn about Indian people today. Wounded Knee and Sand Creek are over, not forgotten, just over, and largely irrelevant to most Indian people. The appalling history is true, but as Bob Roessel would say to his audience, "The point of education about and for Indian people today is now."

THE CONTENT FOR TEACHING ABOUT NATIVE PEOPLES

Begin with the naming question. Some people claim the term "Indian" came from Christopher Columbus when he thought he had landed in India and saw the natives. Some people claim the term "Indian" is demeaning to native peoples. Some people prefer the term "Native American" because, some people claim, it is not demeaning.

Most native peoples in the United States refer to themselves and each other, generically, as Indian and Indians, though among themselves, they prefer tribal names such as Muckleshoot, Hualapai, Chickasaw, Apache, and in the latter case, specifically: Jicarilla, Mescalero, White Mountain, or San Carlos.

There is a history that tells about when Columbus arrived in what became known as "the Americas." There is conflicting evidence regarding whether the Asian subcontinent was known as India at the time, or as Hindustan (see Figure 8.1), or whether the entire landmass in that part of the world was known generically as the "Mogul Empire" (see Figure 8.2).

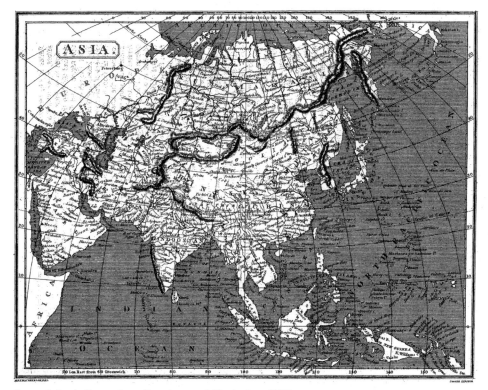

Figure 8.1. Indian subcontinent named Hindustan, 1570.

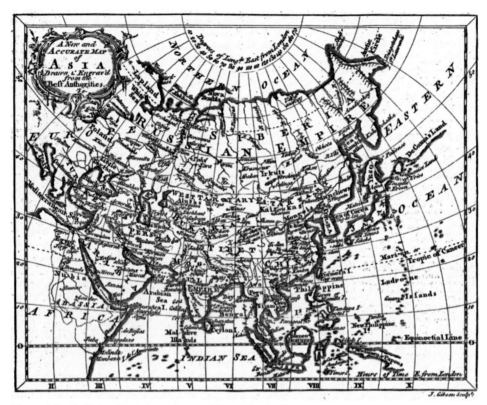

Figure 8.2.   Indian subcontinent named Mogul Empire, 1771.

However, the evidence is not conflicting with regard to how Columbus referred to the natives in his diary. He wrote that he thought the natives he met were beautiful or pretty people, *dios*, perhaps, as in *godlike: dios*, or *indios*—Indian. Look at some references that clarify the naming question.

1. Fernandez-Armesto (1987, 223–230) reported several references to what the natives were called by Columbus, and those who recorded his and others' words at the time: indigenous, man, noble, pretty, aboriginal, natives, savages, and pagan primitives. There is no reference to "American Indians," or "Indians."

2. Fernandez-Armesto (1974, 42) refers to Bartolome de Las Casas' ("scribe" and biographer) report that God had ordained the "discovery" so that "the Indians" could hear His word.

    Bartolome de Las Casas later wrote (1530s) regarding Columbus' journal from November 1, 1492, "It is certain, says the admiral, that this is the mainland, and that I am off Zayton and Quinsay [Shanghai and Hangchow today, both Chinese ports], 100 leagues [approximately 300 miles] distant more or less from the one and the other."

In fact, Columbus didn't know where he was, for he also referred to his location as near "Cipangu," the ancient name for Japan, in which case, he still thought he was off the coast of China and had bumped into Japan there. He did not think he had landed in anything like the Americas, because he was using Marco Polo's maps, which did not include a landmass between Europe and Asia.

If Columbus referred to the people he saw with terminology connected with where he thought he was, he certainly would not have called them "Indians."

3. In Weatherford (2004, 254): "Since he (Columbus) had not found the land of the Great Khan of the Mongols, he decided that the people he met must be the southern neighbors of the Mongols in India, and thus Columbus called the native people of these Americas 'Indians,' the name by which they have been known ever since."

4. Finally, in *The Columbia History of the World* (Garraty and Gay 1972, 629), the authors wrote that the chronology of Indian (India) history reveals that the use of the name "India," as a specific location, dates from the seventeenth century, and between 1500 and 1750 what we know as "India," the land mass south of Tibet, east of the Arabian Sea, west of the Bay of Bengal, was known as the Mughal Empire (to the north), and Ahmadnagar, Golconda, Bidar, and Bijapur, all south of the Mughal Empire. There is no reference to "India" on the pre-1750 map in Garraty and Gay. Nor is that landmass referred to as "India" in maps dated 1560 and 1771 (see Figures 8.1 and 8.2).

What we do know for certain is that neither "Indian" nor "Native American" came from native peoples, themselves. The U.S. Bureau of the Census needed terminology to distinguish among native peoples in the South Pacific, Alaska, and the lower forty-eight. They came up with "Alaska Native," "Pacific Islander," and "Native American," respectively.

We also know that whoever coined the term "Indian," and for whatever reason, it is the term of choice among Indian people today. Among themselves, they use tribal names because they know everyone can distinguish between Standing Rock and Rosebud, Fort Peck and Fort Defiance. But they also know that not one non-Indian in a hundred outside of Montana knows Fort Peck. So they use "Indian."

"Native American" has gotten some traction over the last two decades and reflects the Indian-as-pejorative myth. The website for a recent conference of the Southern California American Indian Resource Center (SCAIR 2010) refers to native peoples sixty-seven times, of which two references are to "indigenous," three to "Native American Indian," seven to "Native American," and fifty-five to "Indian." On that site, they name seventeen separate tribal groups from eight states.

There is no call here for what name to use in reference to native peoples in the United States. Indian people seem not to care much what non-Indians call them. They seem not to care much about what basketball teams put on their jerseys, either. The controversy over tribal names for mascots is largely for and about non-Indians.

BASIC PRINCIPLES FOR INSTRUCTION ABOUT INDIAN PEOPLE

Let us stipulate that everything got renamed and re-owned by the latest arrivers. No one discovered anything. It was all here, and when human beings arrived wherever "here" was, they made it their own.

Let us stipulate that latest-arriving humans took what they wanted from whomever was wherever they happened to wander throughout the 14,000 to 15,000 years between human arrival in what became the Americas (Pringle 2011, 38) and the recent arrival of Columbian explorers. For most of those 14,000–15,000 years everyone was a native, in turn, and they all eventually replaced old natives with new natives who would be replaced again and again by newer natives.

Who *are* the people to whom we refer as "natives," or Indians today? Think about what makes a people who they are. Learn about a group of indigenous people that way. Who are the Paiute, Blackfeet, Metlakatla, and Cree today? Where do Chickasaw, Choctaw, and Chemehuevi peoples live today, what do they do for a living, where do they go to school, and is it possible to connect with children of a selected tribe whose ages are sufficiently similar to our students to set up electronic conversations?

Non-Indian children can learn that the days of oatmeal box drums, acorn mush, grocery-bag "Native American" vests, and headdress are over. Indian people's drums do not sound like they are made from cereal boxes with balloon rubber for drumheads. There isn't one Indian child in a thousand who would eat acorn mush when a hamburger is available. Indian children do not wear vests, and headdress is likely the $100 Stetson worn by every male at a Spearfish, South Dakota, or Gallup, New Mexico, rodeo. Children today need to know that Mohawk means iron-walkers not haircuts, that Navajos may have turned the tide in the war in the Pacific, and that the steelhead trout we eat in an Illinois restaurant may have been in the Quinault River ten hours ago.

The focus when we teach about Indian people is not *how* we teach, but *what* we teach. We teach history, geography, and biography. And if we know enough, we teach economics, government, and religions.

THE RIGHT TO BE WRONG

Many years ago, in its war on poverty, the U.S. Office of Economic Opportunity initiated a program called "Community Action." Included in Community Action

Programs (CAP) were early childhood education (Head Start), housing programs, job training, food banks, medical and dental care, and other efforts designed to blunt the effects and lift people out of the pressures of crushing poverty. CAP's motto was "maximum feasible involvement of the poor in the solution of their own problems."

CAP was less than successful in some situations, largely successful in many, and wildly successful in others. Indian Community Action was wildly successful, and its success over the decades changed Indian America dramatically.

Indian Community Action was initially successful because Indian people are community people. From the beginning, Indian people knew community action better than anyone else. One of the aspects of Community Action Indian people understood perfectly was being in charge of the action in the community, and they understood that being in charge means making decisions.

Good decision makers recognize that decisions have two characteristics (Axelrod 2006, 6). One, decisions are between two or more alternatives or possibilities, and the greater the decision, the higher the stakes of the alternatives. Two, faced with conflicting alternatives or possibilities, a decision *must* be made. While *having* to decide is difficult, not being in the position to decide is worse.

Indian people welcomed the responsibility to decide, and when non-Indians acted out their need to protect Indian people from themselves, Indian people rose up. "We have a right to be wrong" was the primal scream of a people breaking free from two centuries of domination.

If there is no such right to be wrong, people are not in charge. Indian people knew that from the start, and they knew, and have always known, that for as long as non-Indian government protects them from error, they are wards of non-Indian government.

Indian people refer to not being in charge as BIA, and they do not mean Bureau of Indian Affairs. They mean Batting Indians Around. Their conception of BIA comes up when non-Indian people think they can decide what Indian people shall be called, where they shall live, with whom and by whom they shall be schooled, and what Indian people should find insulting.

Beginning in the middle of the last century Indian people began to take charge. CAPs in the 1960s and 1970s stoked the fires of independence, but the fires were started in earnest long before. Interactions between Indian people and non-Indians were no longer with weapons. By the middle of the twentieth century, those interactions were about brainpower and commitment. The playing field was leveled and Indian people began reconstructing their lives on their own terms.

At the end of World War II, every Navajo child who attended school was in a classroom under the direction of the federal government, a state government, or a church. Then in 1967, one year after the initial experiment in Navajo community education in Lukachukai, Arizona, the Navajo Tribe opened its first tribal school in Rough Rock, Arizona. The first Navajo Community School, run entirely by the tribe, progressed in stages from the elementary grades to K–8, and then K–12. The tribe opened its community college in 1968 and graduated its first four-year students, in partnership with Arizona State University, in 1998.

There were nearly three-dozen tribal colleges in the United States as the twenty-first century opened, and today there are countless tribal elementary schools. The tribes have a long way to go, but they are moving now, on their own, in the contemporary world. It has always been an insult to teach about Indian people as though they are a people apart, anthropological subjects without influence, mere victims of colonialism, living in movies and on television screens.

SEPARATE NATION STATUS

"Separate nation status" is a somewhat loose term that goes back to three Supreme Court rulings between 1823 and 1832. So important were the three rulings that when Andrew Jackson was elected president in 1824 and stood in favor of the Indian Removal Act of 1830, in conflict with the Marshall rulings, Jackson remarked derisively that he (Marshall) made his ruling; now let him try to enforce it.

In *Cherokee Nation v. Georgia*, 1831, Cherokees requested relief from particular laws passed by the State of Georgia, which the tribe determined violated its sovereignty. The Court ruled that the tribe is not sovereign, as in a foreign nation, and ruled against the tribe. However, the Court also recognized in its ruling that the tribe has a right to protection, and the United States rightfully has that responsibility.

The question before the Court in *Worcester v. Georgia*, 1832, was whether the State of Georgia had the right to enforce its laws regarding interactions between the State and the Cherokee Nation. The Court ruled no, the State had no such right. The "separation" to which "separate nation status" refers, therefore, is from state jurisdiction in favor of federal jurisdiction.

Beginning in 1832, eighteen decades ago, native peoples in the United States could live on land owned by the United States for Indian occupation and use, in perpetuity. The relationship between Indian tribes and the United States is one of trust, where "trust" means protection by the United States. It means that Indian peoples' and tribes' legal interactions are with the United States, not any state within the United States.

For the story of federal Indian law, see Jaeger (2007) that reports on 400 years of legal interactions between Indian tribes and both European colonies and the United States among 550 federally recognized tribes in the United States.

NATIVE PEOPLES AND SOCIAL STUDIES CONTENT

Everything comes back, as General Dwight David Eisenhower observed, to geography. For content when we teach about native peoples, we begin there.

Think of southwest Colorado, not far from Durango, about fifty miles from where Utah, Arizona, New Mexico, and Colorado come together to form what we know as "Four Corners." In that general area is a historical monument, a national park known as Mesa Verde.

Geography starts at Mesa Verde because the people who lived there, and left suddenly for reasons no one has been able to determine, built similar villages on flat land along what we know as the Rio Grande River, to just a few miles south of where Albuquerque is today and then west to what became the border of Arizona and New Mexico on the edge of where Navajos lived. But they did not stop there. Some of them went into what became Northeast Arizona and settled on the top of three mesas.

We know those people from Mesa Verde built nineteen villages along the river and west into what became Arizona, and we know they did it around a thousand years ago because one of those villages (Old Oraibi) on top of one of those mesas in Arizona is dated at 1100 CE. The people there are called Hopis. They live in pueblos. The villages along the river and west to Arizona are also pueblos and the people are called Santo Domingo, Nambe, Isleta, Acoma, Laguna, and Zuni, to name six of the nineteen.

Here are five geography topics associated with the story of Mesa Verde, the people who suddenly left Mesa Verde, and where they went. These topics are informed by the work of Stephen Cunha (2010).

1. What can we learn about why people from Mesa Verde left their mountainside villages?
2. What can we learn about why those people settled in so many villages along the river?
3. What can we learn about how the people supplied their needs in their new villages?
4. What can we learn about how the people adjusted to and changed their new environments?
5. What can we learn about the Mesa Verde people who headed west and into Navajo country?

Those are geography questions in the context of the study of Indian people. The questions apply to all groups of Indian people over the last several hundred years. How did Cherokee get to Oklahoma? (Question 1) How did Makah, Quileute, and Quinault supply their needs? (Question 3)

History is another content area in the study of Indian people. At about the time when the North and South were fighting it out to see which would destroy the economy of the other, or own human beings, whichever is the preferred rationale, there was another military engagement that involved U.S. troops far to the west of the Mississippi.

In what would become the State of Oregon in 1859, there lived an Indian tribe known as Nez Perce. It is impossible to know how far back the Nez Perce go, but we do know from human artifacts that humans lived in that area as many as 10,000 years ago. Human artifacts that date back that far have been found along the coast of Washington, as well. The oldest Egyptian pyramids date back about 5,000 to 6,000 years.

One hundred fifty years ago, there occurred a battle of retreat during which the Nez Perce, under the leadership of Joseph, son of Joseph before him, led approximately 800 people on a 1,700-mile trek through Idaho, Montana, and portions of Yellowstone, outmaneuvering several pursuing groups of U.S. soldiers, and finally being caught forty miles from the safety of Canada. At Joseph's surrender, he delivered one of the most famous of Indian orations. We know it as "I will fight no more forever." Chief Joseph died in northeast Washington in 1904.

There is a lot of locational geography in the story: Idaho, Washington, Oregon, Montana, Yellowstone, Oklahoma, the North, the South, Egypt, Peru, and China. There is reference to another Indian tribe (Makah) in Neah Bay, Washington. And there is migration, in this case forced migration.

Cherokee were forced to migrate from Georgia and North Carolina to Oklahoma. The story of the march is written in John Ehle's *Trail of Tears*.

Approximately 8,000 Navajo were forced to move from their vast homeland to the Bosque Redondo Reservation in eastern New Mexico in the high desert winter. At the disease-ridden Bosque Redondo Reservation, many Navajo people were lost. But some of the Navajos escaped the march. Under the direction of Navajo War Chief Manuelito, many Navajos marched deep into Canyon del Muerto. This all happened in the mid-1860s, the era of the U.S. Civil War.

Much of what makes people historically literate is knowing enough to "see" history vertically as well as horizontally. We know that the U.S. Civil War occurred between 1861 and 1865. What do we know about Indian America during those years? That could be the history strand in the study of native peoples.

We have written several times in this book that native peoples had, and have, names, thoughts, and ideas, and they spoke. There is no useful "Native American" unit if the people in it, like the horses they used to carry their stuff, have no names, no ideas, and no talk. Biography gives human texture to instruction about native peoples.

There are hundreds of named native people who influenced history. Leaf through the James Curtis (2001) anthology of photographs and brief commentary or a James Kavanaugh collection (1996) to appreciate the simple dictum that Indian people have names. Before you do, however, make a list of Indian people's names. Take one minute and see how many you can put on a list. Then, open a Curtis or Kavanaugh collection and see if you included on your list Left Hand

(Comanche), John Abbott (Osage), Big Knife (Flathead), Bear Bull (Blackfoot), or Chief Hector (Assiniboine).

The point here is not that there are names every culturally literate person should know. The point is that our students should know that Indian people have names, and they had names a century ago, and two centuries ago, and three and four, and the names are just as knowable, and worthy of knowing, as are Marco Polo, Johannes Gutenberg, Genghis Khan, and Martin Luther.

But Gutenberg and Luther were major historical figures who made a difference. We know them because they changed the world. What did Chief Hector do? If we do not know, we cannot know how, if at all, he is worthy of study. In fact, we know who people are *because* of what they did. If that were not the case, no one would know Thomas Edison, Luther Burbank, Benjamin Banneker, or Steve Jobs, for that matter. We know Crispus Attucks because of his appearance at the Boston Massacre. We study biographies of Indian people to learn what Indian people did to make them memorable.

We selected eight people specifically relevant to the geography and history commentaries in this chapter, four of whom are significant Indian people of the last two hundred years.

Sequoyah, Cherokee, had the idea that what Cherokee people said could be recorded and saved. He worked on his idea for many years and came up with an alphabet of eighty-six symbols to record the Cherokee language.

John Ross was leader of the Cherokee nation between 1826 and 1866. He led the Cherokee people on their Trail of Tears from North Carolina and Georgia to Oklahoma, and he led Cherokee delegations in agreements with the Confederate States of America.

Manuelito was the Navajo warrior who led many campaigns against the United States and its attempts to control Navajo people and dictate where they shall live. Born around 1818, he was the commander who led Navajo warriors, women, and children into Canyon de Muerto.

Chief Joseph of the Nez Perce led the last remnants of his people on the famous attempted escape to Canada. His tribe was one of those Lewis and Clark found in their exploration of the Louisiana Purchase.

John Collier, Commissioner of Indian Affairs in the U.S. Department of the Interior between 1933 and 1945, tried to reverse the policy of "assimilation." The policy failed, mostly because no matter how "assimilated" Indian people became, in the view of non-Indians, they were still Indians.

George Boldt, federal court judge, ruled in 1974 that Indian tribes primarily on the Olympic Peninsula were granted fishing rights "at all usual and accustomed grounds and stations." Judge Boldt ruled that treaties shall be honored.

Andrew Jackson, seventh president of the United States, is known for, among other acts, his policy of "Indian Removal." The policy, in general, meant that Indian people shall be removed and relocated to "Indian Territory" west of the Mississippi.

APPLICATIONS FOR THE CLASSROOM

Table 8.1. Sample Lesson Segment, Primary Grades

Objective: Primary grade students will learn the names of at least two native people, their tribal affiliation(s), and their geographic location(s) in the United States.	*Common Core Standards*: Ask and answer such questions as *who* and *where* for the purpose of accumulating knowledge about specific native peoples Write information about *who* and *where* in sentences.

Background: Few students in the primary grades know the name(s) of native peoples, with the exception of Pocahontas and Geronimo. Those are a good start, for both are historically verifiable people. Both have tribal affiliation and geographic location. We refer to Pocahontas and Geronimo to begin the study.	*Vocabulary*: *Tribe*: When people of various similarities gather together, their groups are called clans, clubs, organizations, families, and so forth. Indian people gather in tribes. *Biography*: Story(ies) about the life of a person. "Your biography, Timmy, is the story of your life."	*Comprehensibility and Accessibility*: It is almost certain that few, if any, students bring prior knowledge to the lesson segment(s). Comprehensibility, therefore, does not involve scaffolding for prior knowledge. Much of the information, both print and electronic, will require the same support required when we teach other "February" biographies. Thus, as we teach George Washington and Abraham Lincoln, we use the same support systems when we include Annie Dodge and Standing Bear.

Procedures: We approach Presidents' Month with the intent to leave second graders with a sense of who George Washington and Abraham Lincoln are, with regard to general appearance, location, and principal achievement(s). We include in the month's biographical work Annie Dodge (Navajo, Arizona) and Standing Bear (Assiniboine, Montana). Images of Washington and Lincoln are readily available. Images of Annie Dodge and Standing Bear are readily available on the Internet. Enter their names, and there is as much material available to teach as much about the Indian people as we teach about the presidents, as prior knowledge for later more in-depth instruction.	*Review and Assessment*: Second graders write four sentences, one each about each of the four people included in the February biography unit. The students will respond to the following prompt. "Think of a sentence that includes the name of the Indian woman (Annie Dodge) we studied and either where she lived, her tribe, or what she did." The assessment criterion is accurate information arranged in a sentence.

Table 8.2. Sample Lesson Segment, Intermediate Grades

Objective: Fourth graders will locate tribal groups throughout the continental United States. The students will come to recognize that there are tribal groups in every state, and that there are tribal groups about whom they have never heard.	*Common Core Standards*: Read and comprehend informational texts. Integrate information from several sources on the same topic.

Background: It is unlikely that fourth graders bring very much relevant prior knowledge to this task. They probably know the names of tribal groups in their general neighborhood (state or region), but a sense of tribal groups across the United States is almost certain to be new for them. The scaffolding necessary is simplification of location and, in some cases, perhaps, orientation to Web search.	*Vocabulary*: Compass directions: Northeast, Southeast, Southwest, Northwest, Upper Midwest, Lower Midwest. Almost all tribal names will be new. Pronunciation will be the primary teacher task, with names such as Haulapai (wall uh pie), Quileute (quill e ute), Miccosukee (mick uh sookie), and so forth.	*Comprehensibility and Accessibility*: To accomplish comprehensibility, we first divide the continental United States into six pieces so fourth graders can search in smaller regions. Furthermore, fourth graders need only find 8-12 tribal groups in their region. The task is to recognize that tribal groups of great variety live in their assigned region. It is the image of tribal groups, and their names, which is central in this lesson segment.

Procedures: We view the continental United States as a rectangle, with protrusions for Maine, Florida, and Texas, and the Southwest corner cut off. We draw a horizontal line from Virginia west through the middle of Nevada and to the Pacific coast. We draw a perpendicular line from the southern Arizona/New Mexico border to Canada where western Montana and eastern Idaho meet. We draw another perpendicular line up the Mississippi River from New Orleans to northern Minnesota at Lake Superior. We label the northwest corner "A," upper Midwest "B," Michigan east "C," southeast "D," lower Midwest "E," and southwest "F." There are six areas and six groups of fourth graders. The students' task is to name as few as eight and no more than twelve tribal groups that have tribal lands within their assigned region of the continental United States.	*Review and Assessment*: The teacher conducts on-going assessment by walking around, often referred to as "kid-watching." The informal assessment informs the teacher's individualized attention during subsequent searches. More formal assessment occurs when the searches are finished and each group prepares to participate in an "Indian Tribal Location Faire" in which students separate into six new groups (one member from each former group) to report on their findings.

Table 8.3. Sample Lesson Segment, Middle Levels

Objective: Sixth graders browse both print and electronic sources and accumulate images and ideas about Indian people in biographical, economic, geographic, and historical perspectives. The students select one tribal group at least 500 miles from where the students live. The students write a response to their reading. The topic is "Knowing (tribal name) geographically and historically." Or "biographically and historically" or "economically and geographically," and so forth.	*Common Core Standards*: Draw on information from both print and electronic sources to solve a problem. Summarize from written text.

Background: The sixth graders have written to three reader response prompts for several months. They know how to think in and write the prompts: This is what I noticed, This is what it reminds me of, This is how it makes me feel. They know how to takes reader response notes as they browse and read.	*Vocabulary*: We will have to clarify what the response titles mean: "historical, economic, biographical, geographic perspectives." The students will practice the four perspectives in response to teacher read-alouds from the sixth grade literature canon.	*Comprehensibility and Accessibility*: Those students whose literacy (reading) capacities are not sufficient to browse and read effectively will be provided a reading buddy who will help target students to accumulate the information necessary. The reading buddy will also take dictation from less able students' Reader Responses.

Procedures: This lesson segment will require at least four sessions of 30-45 minutes. The students may work in pairs, but not threes or more, and each student must write his or her own Reader Response. The teacher circulates around the room to respond to questions and clarifications and to help students access electronic sites. This work belongs to the students, however. They must plan their writing based on their own notes, and they must identify the tribal focus and which of the four perspectives they will feature. The students have had direct instruction in the sort of writing in this lesson segment, with sufficient practice. The reading and browsing, and the writing, should require little or no teacher input.	*Review and Assessment*: The students' response to their reading and browsing will fall into two categories, perhaps outlines: This is what I noticed, and This is what it reminds me of. The written pieces will be no fewer than 100 words and not longer than 150 words. Scoring criteria include writing in sentences, organizing into at least two paragraphs, and addressing two of the four areas of focus.

REFERENCES

Axelrod, Alan. 2006. *Profiles in Audacity: Great Decisions and How They Were Made.* New York: Sterling Publishing.

Cunha, Stephen F. 2010. *California: A Changing State, An Atlas for California Students.* Eureka, CA: Humboldt State University, California Geographic Alliance.

Curtis, Edward S., 2001. *The North American Indian: The Complete Portfolios.* Koln, Germany: Taschen.

Deloria, Vine, Jr., 1969. *Custer Died for Your Sins: An Indian Manifesto.* New York: Macmillan.

Fernandez-Armesto, Felipe. 1974. *Columbus and the Conquest of the Impossible.* London: Phoenix Press.

———. 1987. *Before Columbus: Exploration and Colonization from the Mediterranean to the Atlantic, 1229–1492.* Philadelphia: University of Pennsylvania Press.

Garraty, John A., and Peter Gay. 1972. *The Columbia History of the World.* New York: Harper and Row.

Jaeger, Lisa. 2007. *Tribal Nations: The Story of Federal Indian Law.* Fairbanks, AK: Tanana Chiefs Conference.

Kavanaugh, Thomas. 1996. *North American Indian Portraits.* New York: Koneky and Koneky.

Pringle, Heather. 2011. "The First Americans." *Scientific American* 305 (5): 36–45.

SCAIR. 2010. Workshop in Preparation for the U.S. Census, Palm Spring, CA.

Weatherford, Jack. 2004. *Genghis Khan and the Making of the Modern World.* New York: Crown Publishers.

CHAPTER 9

Media Literacy: Radio, Television, and Print Media as Social Studies Text

Learning to Be Informed

This chapter rests on the proposition that much of what is studied in K–8 social studies appears in the daily newspaper and both news and public affairs on radio and television. And all of what appears in the print and electronic media also appears on the Internet. Therefore, much of what appears in the daily newspaper and both news and public affairs on radio and television could be primary textual material in the social studies. Of the many advantages of using media as social studies text, two stand out. One, students could experience social studies content (history, personal finance, civics, and so forth) in the context of their "now." And two, students would have to learn how to use the daily newspaper and both news and public affairs on radio and television as sources of social studies information.

We are not the only people to see the bumper sticker that reads: "Don't believe the liberal media," and the liberal media is all media with which the driver of the car does not agree. We are not alone in being familiar with "niche" radio, television, and print media, where airtime and newsprint are directed to audiences with certain preconceptions, audiences that have prejudged political, economic, and social topics. Those people seek media that feature their own prejudgments. If our students do not learn how to read, watch, and listen to such media, our students cannot be informed by that media.

Leo Tolstoy remarked that the most powerful weapon against ignorance is diffusion of printed material (Leo Tolstoy, in the epilogue to *War and Peace*). But readers of that print material who cannot recognize literary devices designed to confuse, misdirect, and/or misinform gain little.

THE CONTENT FOR TEACHING MEDIA LITERACY

Consider three men walking the same road (Nabokov 2009, 81). One lives in the city, knows precisely where he is and where he is going, and along the way sees everything for what it is—plants, animals, and buildings. Two is a scientist who sees everything in taxonomic terms, observes rather than sees, and records for later study. Three lives along the road, was raised on the land, and tills the fields.

All three men are honest and objective, and each of the three will report on the walk along the road in a way that differs from the other two. The closest the three will come to a common report is that there was a road in the country. Which of the three reports is objective? Which of the three reporters intends to deceive? Which of the three reports is accurate? Are there three "sides" to the observations? If the television channel that reports on the walk in the country reports two sides, is the report unbiased?

Media critics tell us that we begin to solve the bias problem when we purposely present "both sides." Ohio's *Dayton Daily News* offers its promise to balance points of view. Their printed promise reads as follows. "Fairness and balance are critical to our work. You've told us that, and we respect your views. And we've designed our Ideas and Voices pages to consistently provide a balanced offering of commentary from both conservative and liberal columnists and cartoonists."

The *Dayton Daily News* then shows a seven-day chart that features columnists "From the Left" and "From the Right," with both left and right every day. Four of the eleven names on the chart are Robert Reich, Michelle Malkin, Thomas Sowell, and Gail Collins. Regular newspaper readers are able to place the four into the *Daily News'* two categories. There are no Libertarians on the *Daily News'* list of eleven columnists, no socialists, and no independents.

Do we get unbiased commentary from the *Dayton Daily News* editorial pages? In fact, the newspaper does not promise freedom from bias; it promises to balance the bias. We can make a good argument that not only does the newspaper fail to avoid bias; it also fails to provide balance, given that "balance" cannot mean merely two kinds of columnists, especially if there are three kinds, five, or seven. And there certainly are more than two on just about every controversy that matters. That is what our students have to understand.

If the purpose of getting all sides in a story is to have an informed view based on all the sides, what is the informed view? Who decides which report on Nabokov's walk in the country to emphasize, and is that decision objective? Students need to learn how to think that way.

Our students also have to use history, geography, and their Constitution not only to better understand what they see, hear, and read in the media but also to enhance their historical, geographic, and constitutional literacy. Newspaper, radio, and television news make relentless demands on people's prior knowledge, and it is not uncommon that news stories are lost on people without social studies content.

Skilled readers, listeners, and watchers can be informed by print and electronic media. Everyone, including students, can learn the skills. Our students have to know how media influences readers, listeners, and watchers. It is not so much that the media is skewed; it is more that consumers of media do not know how they are being influenced. We can teach our students to ask whether there is a different perspective on what they read. They can learn to ask if two "sides" are sufficient. They can learn to wonder how many "sides" there are, and they can learn to think that the question may not be about "sides."

A fall 2012 Gallup poll found that 60 percent of Americans say they have little or no confidence in mass media to report the news fairly and accurately (Pareene 2012, 146).

What if those Americans were right? What if the news is bad, and the writers and reporters lie? What if people want truth and good news, but there isn't any in radio, television, and newspaper stories? What if social studies textbooks are not complete because there isn't page space for everything, so writers and editors select what will be included, which means they select what will not be included, and that means their biases control what students learn?

Textbook writers do have their own ideas about what is true, and their editors may influence what will and what will not be selected. Political and social pressure groups do influence who and what appears in social studies textbooks. That does not mean the books lie. Responsible teachers, who also have their political and social perspectives, teach students how to read textbooks as critical thinkers. This is the point at which we must define some terms on which critical reading and thinking can rest.

MEDIA LITERACY

Teachers record a drive-time radio-talker to play, commercial-free, twice per week in their social studies classes. Students' task is to identify fallacies and propaganda, with particular attention to guilt by association, consistency, straw men, name-calling, and the big lie. Those five were selected for study because their continual use tends to make them seem normal. "Repeat something often enough and it begins to appear normal" is a variation on an epigram about propaganda. Teachers begin with definitions and examples drawn from electronic and print media.

In a recording of a radio-talker (EIB Radio July 25, 1996, 9:05–9:15 a.m. PST segment), the host committed eight minutes to a *Time* magazine cover photograph of a presidential candidate with a printed caption, "Is _____ too old to run for president?" During the monologue, the host referred to a "biased" media that said the candidate is too old. In the magazine story, it was reported that *Time*'s poll showed most people do not think the candidate is too old to run for president. Just before the commercial, the host said, again, "*Time* says _____'s too old."

Fifth graders listened to the radio segment and in a follow-up discussion remarked that *Time* said nothing like what the host said, but the host kept saying it, so his closing statement before the commercial sounded accurate. For the students, the object lesson was a perfect example of the "big lie." They detected it immediately thereafter when it appeared in both print and electronic media. When we teach it, in media context, students learn to recognize it, and they become increasingly informed and critical readers and listeners.

A class of seventh graders, to a person, was familiar with the phrase, "liberal media." They listened to a recording of an August 31, 1995, drive-time radio-talker (8:32 a.m., PST) who reported that the owner of a local "liberal" metropolitan newspaper gave one-half million dollars to an upcoming presidential convention. It was just one line in several minutes of monologue about a huge convention coming to the city. The seventh graders listened to the recording of the morning radio monologue from a decade before, in response to which they were to note the existence, if any, of bias.

They found no instances of bias in the ten-minute recording, but seventeen of the twenty-two seventh graders wondered why the local newspaper is called "liberal" when its owner just gave a one-half million dollars to the convention of a seemingly opposing party. Those seventh graders had been in four fifteen-minute sessions of both print and electronic media literacy in a social studies class. They posed a critical question after a mere sixty minutes of experience with critical listening.

When a news story argues against an idea because it comes from someone whose background is suspect, the writer of the story is guilty of an *ad hominem* argument. The report is about an officeholder's position against farm subsidies. The report tells readers or listeners that the officeholder never worked on a farm, never owned farmland, and has never tried to sell corn on Chicago's commodities market.

The report includes commentary about the suburban home in which she grew up, the rich suburban public school she attended, and the Ivy League university from which she graduated. It emphasizes that the officeholder never drove a tractor and never lived in a corn-growing state. The report further points out that the officeholder's children all went to private schools. Nowhere in the report is there any reference to the merits of the officeholder's perspective on farm subsidies.

Inconsistency is an ad hominem argument. Someone voted for an economic reform package that included raising the eligibility criterion for Social Security. The vote is dismissed in a news story because she had voted for other economic policies that protected the elderly. She is labeled inconsistent and is dismissed. There is no commentary about the merits of her vote for raising eligibility criteria for Social Security. All of the commentary was about her being inconsistent.

There was also no commentary about whether she was, in fact, inconsistent about her two votes.

The editorial page in the local newspaper refers to a political candidate's tax policies as "far right." There is nothing in the editorial about the extent, if any, to which the candidate's tax policies have merit. If our students cannot recognize an ad hominem argument, they won't wonder what "far right" means, or what a "far right" tax policy is as opposed to a "far left" tax policy and what a not-so-far right or left tax policy might be.

Radio and television hosts and columnists in the newspaper routinely avoid the question on the table; rather, they associate the question on the table with something listeners and readers do not like and influence the print and electronic audience to choose rather than think about the topic. Middle school students in media classes find ad hominem arguments virtually every day in media. The point is not to direct students away from the radio and television talkers and newspaper reporters and columnists. The point is to teach them how to listen to and read how hosts and writers manage their audiences.

A *straw man* is an idea or position used for the single purpose of destroying it. It is often a misrepresentation, connected to someone, a perspective, or an agency that needs to be compromised for a political purpose. As we have shown, there can be no objective or bias-free media. The charge of bias is, therefore, a straw man, used to compromise the value of media as an informing agent in the society.

A prime example of the straw man occurred several decades ago. The straw man term was "national malaise," a term used to characterize a time frame, not Americans, but it was highlighted and connected to a man, and then the man was criticized relentlessly for his association with the term. The man will wear the term forever.

Another common straw man is the argument that people who want to legislate against certain firearms and ammunition in private hands fail to remember that the first thing a legendary Central European dictator did was to disarm the citizens. The argument allows people to destroy the firearm and ammunition argument by aligning it with the dictator's take-over of his country.

A *red herring* is a distraction of attention from the question on the table. A customer at a restaurant tells a waiter that the coffee is not hot, and the waiter says the coffeemaker has been acting up. The question is tepid coffee. That the coffeemaker has been acting up is a distraction from the fact that the coffee is not hot. The waiter and customer could have a scintillating conversation about coffeemakers, while the coffee is still tepid.

A bond issue to fix decaying streets and install two traffic lights is on the table in a small South Dakota town. At a town meeting, a citizen tells her friends and neighbors that she understands the town needs to fix the streets and install traffic lights, "but," she says, "we are being taxed to death, and there has to be a stop to it all." There follows heated discussion about taxes, and at the time-certain 9:00 adjournment, no progress was made on the bond issue because the whole town spent ninety minutes talking about how much they are taxed.

The larger tax burden for citizens in the small South Dakota town is a red herring, a distraction from the question on the table. When we read commentary in the newspaper regarding what to do about immigration, and the commentary focuses on whether or not unemployed citizens would do the work the immigrants do, we have a red herring. The question is what do we do about immigration, and we fail to address the question for as long as we talk about stoop labor. Both of those topics may be important, but neither addresses the question of what to do about immigration.

An important part of media literacy is knowing what to look for when we read and listen. Another part is sufficient general knowledge to know fallacious reasoning when it appears. If we know what each branch of our government is responsible for doing, for example, we know that a report that the president is taxing citizens out of their savings is fallacious because presidents don't have taxation authority.

We know that criticism of a president for not allowing the generals to conduct a war their way is fallacious because ours is a civilian military, and generals do not conduct wars in the United States.

We also know that there is no reference in the Constitution to all men being created equal. Media literacy rests on general knowledge and the skill to read and listen to media critically. And because media exists in very short segments, mere seconds of news and commentary spots, the general knowledge necessary to be media literate is often at the level of what loaded words mean.

LIBERAL MEDIA

Liberals are said to believe in the sanctity of individual rights and freedom and change by political action. They "feel obliged to try to do something about any and every social problem, to cure every social evil" (Miner 1996, 43–44). Liberals believe in progress by social action and reform by law rather than by revolution. Liberals believe in a balance between free enterprise and government controls. Liberals believe people are essentially good and have a right to equality. Liberals think of watchwords such as "social justice" and "fairness" (Kristol 1995, 257). They believe in intellectual independence and broadmindedness.

The term "progressive" has come to replace the word "liberal." Progressive means to move forward (Krugman 2007, 270). Liberal media, therefore, would feature attributes of free enterprise, with the people's (government) oversight to control the free enterprise economy's tendency to concentrate resources in the hands of a small percentage of the people. Liberal media would support laws that ensure individual rights, personal freedom, and everyone's access to well-being.

CONSERVATIVE MEDIA

Conservative means predisposition to conservation or preservation, even resistance to change (Miner 1996, 64). The term comes from seventeenth-century French (to oppose revolution), and was adopted by England's Tories (maintenance of the traditional order). Conservatism features personal responsibility for the consequences of one's actions. Conservatives think people, rather than government, are better able to assume responsibility. Conservatism is committed to unfettered capitalist principles (Branden 1986, 252).

Conservatism's beginnings are in Edmund Burke's reactions to French philosophers' idealization of reason, the essential goodness of human nature, and creation of an ideal world. Both Barry Goldwater (1960, 12) and Ayn Rand (1957, 411) refer to a conservative "morality," which means the foundations necessary to stand on classical conservative principles, mainly limited government and unfettered free enterprise economy. Ayn Rand eventually rejected conservatives, though not conservatism (Brandon 1986, 252).

Conservative media would value personal responsibility over dependence on others (government). Conservative media would stand for largely unrestrained capitalism. Conservative media's preference for tradition over reason would favor media's story selection and treatment to emphasize greater reliance on traditional values than on social change. *National Review* is a conservative magazine, and it articulates the news of the day according to conservative principles.

LIBERTARIAN MEDIA

Libertarians claim to believe in limited government and the sanctity of the individual's right to make his own choices. Thus the appeal of the libertarian's bumper sticker: "I'm Pro-Choice on Everything."

An exchange about Libertarianism and nationalized health insurance illustrates basic libertarian ideals. When asked who pays for the medical care an uninsured citizen needs, a prominent Libertarian physician and the churches took care of uninsured prospective patients. He remarked, and we paraphrase, no one was ever turned away from hospital care because he wasn't insured.

The Libertarian believes people are responsible for their own behavior and if they are irresponsible, government is not the safety net of last resort. Libertarianism is a nonnegotiable perspective on limited government, where the limits are spelled out in the Constitution. Amendment Ten of our Bill of Rights says, in essence, that whatever is not granted to the federal government in the Constitution is reserved for the states and the people.

Libertarian media would highlight the many instances of federal intrusion into state and individual affairs. Libertarian media would emphasize what the Constitution does authorize for federal management: the census, mail delivery, border protection, and national defense. The magazine *Reason* is libertarian, and its pages explain libertarian positions on issues of the day.

INDEPENDENT MEDIA

There is a broad range of Americans who do not identify with Republican or Democrat, conservative or liberal, libertarian, or anything else. They are independent. Independents tend to refer to themselves as "centrists," or voters who do not place themselves in any major party's camp.

But Independents are probably not so centrist as they are diverse with regard to how they think. They might be economically conservative and socially liberal, or economically socialist and socially liberal. Most think neither Republicans nor Democrats reflect how they think.

Independents claim to cast ballots for individuals rather than parties. Independents are hard to describe, which is what makes them independent. Independent media, unlike liberal and conservative media, is difficult to predict.

Independents are likely to listen to a little liberal radio and a little conservative television and read more than one newspaper, purposely to benefit from different points of view. Of the approximately 20 million listeners that conservative radio claims, for example, it is impossible to know how many Independents tune in just to hear how the controversy of the day is handled by conservative radio talkers.

NONCOMMERCIAL, OR "PUBLIC" MEDIA

Created by Congress in 1967, the Corporation for Public Broadcasting contributes approximately fifteen cents of every dollar necessary to run public radio and television stations. The rest of the public radio and television budget comes from private grants and public giving. There is no commercial income because there are no commercials. A program will show in the beginning or end that "This program was made possible through a grant from ——," and there might be an image of a new automobile or a drug manufacturing plant onscreen when the car or drug company is mentioned, but public radio and television do not sell commercial time.

Public radio and television avoid editorial commentary as news. When there is a one-hour news show, what the public sees and hears is news. It may be that during the show there are interviews with people who talk from a point of view, but those sessions tend to be announced as "roundtables" during which contributors voice their opinions.

Unlike commercial media, viewers and listeners to public radio and television will not hear or see a newsperson promulgate a position or perspective on a political or economic controversy. That does not keep some commercial commentators from charging public radio and television with bias. A station's avoidance of bias is often viewed as a bias.

The trouble with the labels, informing though they might be, is that very few of the people who claim a label in fact behave, or even think and feel, as their label is defined. Many people's labels are little more than reactions to other people's labels, as in, "I'm a Libertarian because Independents are cowards for not taking a stand."

The sort of bias named on the bumper sticker, therefore, often does not reflect a political or economic position. Liberalism might mean nothing other than against conservative. The labels, therefore, often do not mean what people think and believe except that they don't think and believe like the others.

BIAS AND WHAT IT MEANS IN THE MEDIA

What does "bias" mean? Bias, with regard to media, means reporting those portions of a story that fit prejudgments and avoiding those portions of the story that conflict with prejudgments. Bias is not lying; it is selecting.

Every writer is a selection machine. Virtually every word written in the modern English language is contained in the latest edition of the *Random House Webster's College Dictionary*. Writers select from that book which words to use, how many times to use them, and how to arrange them in sentences.

Every idea constructed in the human mind can be perceived in more than one way. Writers cannot perceive and present an idea in all of the possible ways, if only because no one is privy to all the ways. Writers select how they will present every idea they write.

By definition and by the nature of the species, every story and every idea is selected from alternatives. As a species, each of us is imprisoned in how we look at the world, and each of us looks at the world differently. The notion that the presentation of ideas in the media is not an artifact of selection is absurd.

The bias to which most media critics refer is about purposeful selection, designed to deceive. To the question about what bias is, the answer is that it is the natural consequence of being human. It is not clear that there is a plan to deceive in the normal process of selecting news stories and how those news stories are presented. That doesn't mean there isn't such a plan. It means it is hard to determine a plan.

That is why bias in the media is so important. It is important because newspapers, radio, and television (and more recently the Internet) represent the equality on which democracy in America depends. Our students need to learn that the bias is natural, and that the culture of equality in their generation depends on their ability to use media insightfully and critically.

Print and electronic media as social studies text does not avoid bias; *it explains it*. Media as social studies text does not criticize bias; it celebrates our ability to recognize and understand bias. We do not attempt to control bias; we multiply media sources because the more bias there is, the more sources we need. If what has become known as "mainstream media" is biased, we need more of it, not less. If niche media is biased, we need to double the number of niche commentators, not reduce their number.

To sense bias in the media, our students have to know what it looks and sounds like. Our students have to learn how to distinguish between what they read, see, and hear and whom they read, see, and hear. They have to learn how to recognize if and how media outlets are trying to manipulate what and how they think and feel. They have to know that newspapers come in great variety, and they have to read the variety and notice what the variety means. That is what we teach when we teach media as social studies text.

Infusion of current events in the social studies is not merely a weekly report from a newspaper. It is comparing and contrasting the same story from two or more newspapers and from those two newspapers with two or three television or radio stations. It is describing news from the Internet and news from both television and radio. Our students have to hear a story on public radio and television and the same story in commercial print and electronic media.

It is certainly fair to ask where the time comes from. To learn how to read and to watch and listen to the media requires far more time than we routinely commit to current events, and often current events minutes are taken from ever-diminishing social studies time. There is no way to squeeze 350 minutes into a 300-minute school day.

So we find time elsewhere in the school day to read newspapers, watch news reports on television, and listen to news reports and on the radio. If our students are to understand how to determine the nature of how media reports the news, they have to watch, listen to, and read a great deal of media reports of the news. And they must learn to understand, for it is the understanding that makes people effective citizens.

We do not teach our students to read so they can read. We teach them to read so they can read *something*, something that makes a difference in their lives. If reading does not make a difference, reading has no purpose.

Our students have to learn that media with which they agree does not inform them. People are informed because they are skilled as insightful and critical readers, listeners, and watchers of media with which they do and do not agree. We commit sufficient classroom time to critical reading, listening, and watching be-cause that is what makes citizens who can keep the republic.

STUDENTS ENGAGE IN CURRENT EVENTS

To this point, this chapter has been devoted to *what* we can teach our students so they have some tools for reading, listening to, and watching media. However, the foundation for media literacy is reading, watching, and listening to media. "En-gaging" media means action. We want our students actively engaged in talking about what they see, hear, and read.

CREATIVE AND CRITICAL THINKING AND A MEDIA LITERACY MATRIX: GRADE FOUR AND AFTER

"Make a list of current events. You have one minute. Put on your list whatever you think is a current event, from any portion of the newspaper or newscast on radio or television. Go."

As the students make their lists, make a chart on the board. Put an X on the matrix under "Fluency" and to the right of "Make a list." That would be the X at the upper left. The rest of the matrix (shown filled in) is filled in as the procedures that follow unfold.

When one minute ends, direct the students to find a partner. "With your partner, make a master list of five items. Each of you brings a list to the discussion. Now

Table 9.1.   Board Display for Engagement in Current Events

	Fluency	Negotiate	Interpret	Evaluate	Justify	C/C	Talk	Write
Make a list	X							
Dyads ML		X		X	X	X	X	
Dyads RO		X	X		X	X	X	
Fours ML		X		X	X	X	X	
Fours RO		X	X		X	X	X	
Eights ML		X		X	X	X	X	
Eights RO		X	X		X	X	X	
Criteria		X			X		X	
Paragraph		X			X		X	X

you have to work out a way to get the two lists down to one master list of five. You may combine items or eliminate items. You must come out with a master list of five." This usually takes two to three minutes. Give them more if they need it, but not more than another minute.

As they work, put an X on the matrix to the right of "Dyads ML" (Master List) and under "negotiate, evaluate, justify, compare-contrast, and talk." To a greater or lesser degree, those are what the students are doing when they work in dyads to pare their lists to five.

Meander the room and check into each dyad to make sure they have their master list. If they are ready at three minutes, go to the next "round" of the activity. But go after four minutes whether or not they are ready.

"Look over your master list of five items and determine which of the five is most important, then the next most important, the next, and so forth until you have rank-ordered the list of five from most to least important. Determine your own criteria, or rules, for deciding on the importance of the items."

As they make their rank orders, enter an X to the right of "Dyads Rank Order" and under "negotiate, interpret, justify, compare-contrast, talk"; those are what they are doing to accomplish the task.

Then, "Each dyad is to join another dyad to make groups of four." If there is an odd number of dyads, break up one of the dyads so one person goes to one group of four and the other goes to another group of four. "Each dyad brings five items to the group of four, so there is the possibility of ten items in the new group of four. In each group of four, the task is to pare down the items on the table to a master list of four."

During their deliberations, enter an X to the right of "4s Master List" and under "negotiate, evaluate, justify, compare-contrast, and talk." When they have a new master list, direct them to rank order the list. As they rank order their lists, enter X to the right of "4s Rank Order" and under "negotiate, interpret, justify, compare-contrast, talk."

Repeat the master list task in groups of eight, and enter X to the right of "8s Master List" and under "negotiate, evaluate, justify, compare-contrast, and talk." Then assign the rank ordering and enter X to the right of "8s Rank ordering" and under "negotiate, interpret, justify, compare-contrast, talk."

While they are in their groups of eight, direct a new task. They are to write the criteria, or the basis, on which they determined their master lists and their rank orders. That is a one-minute task, at most. To any clarifying question, respond, "It's your game. How did you decide? I can't help you."

The criteria now listed, make the final assignment. "In each group of eight, collaborate on a one-paragraph explanation of your number one item." They need three to five minutes. While they collaborate, enter X to the right of "Paragraph" and under "negotiate, justify, talk, write."

Finally, one member of each group of eight reads aloud the group's criteria and the group's paragraph.

Now to the debrief. Think about the sentence: People tend to learn what they do, not necessarily what they are taught. The question is, what did the students *do*? They brainstormed current events. Then they negotiated (possibly eight times), evaluated (possibly three times), interpreted, justified, compared, contrasted, talked, and wrote—always about current events, always about the current events they decided were important, and always based upon what they determined "important."

Table 9.2.   Sample Lesson Segment, Primary Grades

Objective: First graders are introduced to the newspaper. They will recognize that newspapers are divided into sections, and three of the sections are: Front Page, Sports, and Comics. The teacher will read aloud from each section, and students will respond to reader response questions.	*Common Core Standards*: Identify who is telling the news story. Answer questions about key details in a story.

Background: It is a rare first grader who knows very much about newspapers, and the first grader who has read a newspaper is rarer still. Most first graders have little or no background with the newspaper as a source of information. From teachers' read-alouds and reader response questions, first graders begin to accumulate prior knowledge.	*Vocabulary*: Newspaper: Define by example. Sections of newspapers: Define by example.	*Comprehensibility and Accessibility*: The existence of newspapers in the classroom for a purpose other than protecting floor tiles under painting easels begins the process of comprehensibility and accessibility. Because a prime rationale for systematic reading aloud by teachers is to ensure that everyone in the room has access to the text, the teacher read-alouds and discussion from reader response questions promote accessibility.

Procedures: Bring a local newspaper into the classroom and over several days or weeks show students that there are sections, there are "stories" in each section, and that each section has its own kind of stories. The sports section has stories about games and people. Front pages have stories about world, national, and local news. The comics have stories, and some of the stories appear as images with one-sentence captions below. Teachers show, describe, and read aloud from the three sections of a local newspaper. Read-alouds show that there is information in the newspaper, and first graders can understand some of the information. Over time, bring in other newspapers to show that most towns and cities have their own newspaper, and almost every newspaper has the three sections. Teachers read aloud from a newspaper every day through the year.	*Review and Assessment*: Formal assessment tests on first graders' ability to recognize newspapers and describe three sections in newspapers. Informal assessment rests on students' responses to reader response questions posed after read-alouds from three sections of different newspapers. First graders' responses to questions must show reading comprehension.

Table 9.3. Sample Lesson Segment, Intermediate Grades

Objective: Fourth graders will describe, compare, and contrast news stories from print and electronic media.	*Common Core Standards*: Determine a theme of a story. Use details and examples when describing text. Compare and contrast point of view. Explain major differences between and among media sources.

Background: Fourth graders have previously studied and engaged in distinguishing between fact and opinion in their reading. This lesson segment is an extension on their prior knowledge, applied to electronic and print media.	*Vocabulary*: *Theme or main idea of a news story*: The meaning of "main idea" is extended from students' work with paragraph thinking and writing. *Point of View*: Recognizing that a story reveals the writer as well as the news story.	*Comprehensibility and Accessibility*: In the case of print media, it is important to utilize reading buddies and teacher read-alouds. In the case of radio and television news, no one needs to read at all, but everyone does need to listen actively. Active listening is a necessary part of instructional procedure.

Procedures: The teacher conducts direct instruction regarding describing skills applied to news stories. The best describing skills rest in what students notice in and about news stories and the extent, if any, to which one news story is similar and different as it is reported in more than one source. A t-chart is a useful tool for recording similarities and differences, as fourth graders perceive them in news stories read aloud, or buddy read, and listened to actively on radio and television. Active listening involves concentration, which is promoted as readers and listeners rethink (capture progressively larger main ideas) the stories, at first line-by-line or sentence-by-sentence. Over time, fourth graders begin to understand active listening and are able to rethink in larger chunks of information. They construct main idea(s) from one source on the left of a t-chart, fold the paper to reveal only the right side of the t-chart, and construct main idea(s) as they read or actively listen to another news source on the same story. They compare and contrast their two lists of main ideas, and they compare and contrast their main ideas with other's main ideas. This lesson segment "runs" through the school year, more than one time each week, and it depends on recordings of radio and television news so students can listen to news reports more than once.	*Review and Assessment*: Each experience as described as "Procedures" is a review of describing, comparing, and contrasting news stories from multiple sources. As fourth graders become increasingly effective at careful reading and listening, the teacher can direct them to write two-to-three-sentence pieces that reflect descriptions, comparisons, and differences between and among multiple news reports. Students' writing informs subsequent instruction focused on, perhaps, description, comparing, and/or contrasting or, perhaps, active and critical listening, itself.

Table 9.4. Sample Lesson Segment, Middle Levels

Objective: Seventh graders will learn to identify the existence, if any, of bias in news stories and determine how bias is displayed.	*Common Core Standards*: Describe how a speaker's or writer's point of view influences how events in a news story are described. Cite specific textual evidence to support analysis of primary and secondary sources.

Background: Seventh graders likely have heard about bias or prejudgment over their last several years. The students have relevant prior knowledge. What they do not have is an understanding that knowing the nature of bias is just as important as knowing bias when we see or hear it. This lesson segment capitalizes on existing prior knowledge to teach the nature of bias.	*Vocabulary*: Red Herring, Straw Man, Big Lie, ad Hominem, and Hypocrisy are all defined and described in this chapter. This lesson segment must begin with at least five sessions of approximately 20 minutes during which the five examples of bias are defined and identified in teacher-selected readings and electronic media.	*Comprehensibility and Accessibility*: Most seventh graders are able to understand most media stories, depending on the media outlet. Newspaper readability levels range from what third graders can read comfortably (tabloids) to what tenth graders can read comfortably (*The Wall Street Journal*). Compared with public radio and television news reports and commentary, local media are usually easier for people to understand than is public media. With teacher guidance, this lesson segment makes few demands for literacy support.

Procedures: Teachers define and lead seventh graders to identify the five specific kinds of bias in news stories and commentary. Students share and compare their judgments in pursuit of commonality in identification. Reliability need not be perfect, of course, but the objective is better than chance (even distribution of identifications through the five kinds of bias). With consistent instruction, that includes examples of media pieces that feature biases that range from obvious to less and less obvious, instructional experiences lead students to ever-greater precision at identification and description. Teachers' preparation for this lesson segment is crucial, for they have to select, copy, and record media pieces for instructional use.	*Review and Assessment*: This is on-going, just as is the instruction. Assessment informs subsequent review and instruction. The most important part of this lesson segment is to stay the course. This is difficult material, but year-long attention, perhaps weekly, will habituate not only looking for bias, but noticing its form or nature.

There was also a high probability of accessibility for everyone because the students conducted all the discussions, on the students' terms, and in the students' language forms.

If teachers conduct that activity once per week for the school year, students are likely to be more literate in current events than any others of comparable age.

APPLICATIONS TO THE CLASSROOM

REFERENCES

Branden, Barbara. 1986. *The Passion of Ayn Rand.* Garden City, NY: Doubleday.

Goldwater, Barry. 1960. *The Conscience of a Conservative.* New York: Hillman Books.

Kristol, Irving. 1995. *NeoConservatism: The Autobiography of an Idea.* Chicago: Ivan R. Dee.

Krugman, Paul. 2007. *The Conscience of a Liberal.* New York: W.W. Norton.

Miner, Brad. 1996. *The Concise Conservative Encyclopedia: 200 of the Most Important Ideas, Individuals, Incitements, and Institutions That Have Shaped the Movement.* New York: Free Press.

Nabokov, Vladimir. 2009. "The Metamorphosis." In *The Story about the Story, Great Writers Explore Great Literature.* Edited by J. C. Hallman, 79–114. Portland, OR: Tin House Books.

Pareene, Alex. 2012. "What Dies along with Newspaper," *The Week,* October 5, 2012.

Rand, Ayn. 1957. *Atlas Shrugged.* New York: New American Library.

CHAPTER 10

Writing in the Social Studies

A team of fourth grade teachers agreed to teach five social studies units during the school year. Because writing was a curricular focus in the district, the fourth grade teachers agreed that the formal assessment requirement in each of the five units would be writing. The writing included paragraphs, summaries, narratives, reports of information, opinion essays, journals, and letters written from the perspective of biographical characters in the social studies units.

When the district social studies instructional consultant came to the school to meet with the fourth grade team, she asked the teachers how many of the fourth graders they taught during the last three years knew how to write the formal modes of discourse and genres sufficiently well to write what they knew about the social studies. The teachers recalled recent fourth graders and acknowledged that most could not write that well. But they assured the district consultant that if the students were to write enough, they would eventually write that well.

Ask most fourth graders to write a paragraph about what they know of the geography of their state (typical social studies content in the fourth grade) or about Abraham Lincoln, George Washington, or Martin Luther King Jr. (typical biographical studies), and the first clarifying question from the students will be, "How many sentences do we have to write?" The fourth graders have been taught that sentence count is an attribute of paragraphs.

The next question is likely to be, "Do we have to indent?" Then, "Do we make a list first?" Paragraph instruction began in the second grade, and the fourth graders are posing clarifying questions that have little, if anything, to do with thinking and writing in paragraphs.

We could be accused of overreach here because after all, it is only the fourth grade. Numbers of sentences and architecture (indention) are like training wheels for paragraph writing; students have to start somewhere. That is fair enough. Training wheels are a kind of scaffold, and scaffolding goes back decades to the principle of successive approximation in teaching and learning (Skinner 1953; Pearson and Gallagher, 1983).

But in operant conditioning psychology applied to human learners, scaffolds eventually disappear.

Fourth graders are still counting sentences, and fifth graders, and sixth and ninth because their teachers are still talking to them about numbers and kinds of sentences, and geometric shapes and even similes about fast food ("hamburger" paragraphs).

Paragraph thinking and writing are rarely taught, which is essentially why so few sixth and seventh graders understand paragraph thinking and writing. It is also why even the most earnest social studies students have a hard time writing what they know and understand about social studies, even when they know their social studies.

If thinking and writing in paragraphs, summaries, reports of information, journals, and so forth are assessment tools for social studies learning, students have to learn how to think and write those forms.

We have to rethink *what* we teach when we teach students to write. Most teachers range from good to terrific at *how* to teach, and in writing, many, if not most, teach mostly the wrong stuff often brilliantly. This chapter is about *what* to teach. It is not a writing book, so there are brief descriptions with brief examples. The latest datasets about the influence of what is in this chapter appear as articles in the *Journal of Basic Writing* (Fearn and Farnan 2007) and *Action in Teacher Education* (Fearn and Farnan, 2007). The latest text on the subject is *Interactions: Teaching Writing and the Language Arts* (Fearn and Farnan 2001). We have been referring to paragraph thinking and writing, so we begin there.

THINKING AND WRITING IN PARAGRAPHS

Instruction about paragraph thinking and writing begins without reference to numbers or kinds of sentences, fast food similes, rhyming patterns, geometric shapes, and architectural designs (Fearn and Farnan 2007, 19).

Arranging Sentences: Grades 2–5, and Thereafter, as Needed and Appropriate

Post a sentence for everyone in the room to see and read, if they can, or repeat aloud after the teacher reads. We begin with a four- to five-sentence paragraph with the sentences revealed in random order one at a time. Here is the first sentence.

He signed a paper to make all slaves free.

"What do you think this is about?" Don't bother defining what a paragraph is; it has been clear forever that the ability to define a paragraph (or a sentence, for that matter) isn't related to the ability to write one. Just pose the question, and use the word *paragraph*. Even second graders might volunteer something about freeing the slaves, and by the third grade, someone will name President Lincoln. Take several responses to the question. "Here is another sentence."

He was the sixteenth president of the United States.

"Which of the two sentences do you think should come first?" In fact, both possibilities are plausible. The point of the question is to cause the students to think about how sentences fit in order. Ask again what they think the paragraph might be about. Avoid trying to teach anything. There is nothing to teach. "Now let's read this sentence."

Abraham Lincoln was president during the Civil War.

They do not have to know what the Civil War means. They are merely trying to find a plausible (what sounds right) order for the sentences. Try it. Number the three sentences 1, 2, 3 in order of their appearance. How does 3, 2, 1 sound? How about 3, 1, 2? How about 2, 1, 3? Someone will call out that 3 has to be first because we won't know who "he" is. Someone has started to think in paragraphs.

Writers think that way. They write certain words in certain order to make sentences in certain order and paragraphs in order, and so forth. How do they know? They don't. They just think about all the possibilities, and they choose one. The best writers make the best choices.

He was very tall, and he wore a big black hat.

"Read the paragraph the way you think it should be. Someone read. Charlene?" Charlene reads 3, 2, 4, 1. Maryann reads 3, 2, 1, 4. Emilio reads 3, 1, 2, 4. Then Emilio says 4 isn't right. He just has a sense that 4 doesn't belong.

Some people think Abraham Lincoln saved the United States.

Hands shoot up: 3, 2, 1, 5; 3, 1, 5, 2; 3, 5, 1, 2, 4. "Elizabeth, how about 4 in your paragraph?" Elizabeth says she doesn't like 4 because it doesn't fit. "Okay, no one has to use 4." Hands shoot up again. "Not now. Write the paragraph the way you think it should be. You do not have to use 4, but you may if you like. Your paragraph is your ticket out the door. You have five minutes."

That was the first of the paragraph thinking and writing lessons in your social studies program. There will be another tomorrow and the day after, each time with a different list of three to six sentences, from the social studies book or a biography related to the unit under study. Change the number of sentences with each session. We do not want young writers to get accustomed to paragraphs that have a certain number of sentences.

In the first paragraphing session, all of the students, no matter their ability to speak, read, or write in English have access to the social studies information (Abraham Lincoln). Remember, the paragraph is read again, aloud, one additional sentence at a time. Everyone will get biographical information, which is the point of the lesson, and most everyone will write a paragraph.

Older students might have more complex social studies textual material, and their paragraph thinking and writing is little or no better than that of their second and fourth grade brothers and sisters. We arrange sentences for several days and then move to paragraph sentence cards (Fearn and Farnan 2001, 150–55).

Paragraph Sentence Cards: Grades 2–4, and Thereafter as Needed

Prepare a set of single-sentence cards or strips, the same set for each student in the room. Prepare the sentence cards or strips from an important part of the text-book. Direct the students to arrange the sentences in order. When one asks, "Is this okay?" ask if it works, if it makes sense.

> For a presidential candidate to pledge that
> he would serve only one term was unthinkable.
> He made clear he was speaking for himself, not his party.
> During his administration, President Polk
> increased the United States landmass by one-third.
> He left office after one term.
> He immediately announced that
> he would not be a candidate for reelection.
> James K. Polk was nominated for president in 1844.

The sentences are selected directly from the text, revised for age- and ability-appropriateness and typed in random order, centered, and in type large enough to cover about half the page. The passage is paraphrased from *Polk: The Man Who Transformed the Presidency and America* (Borneman 2008). Each set of six sentence cards or strips is in a separate envelope (or paper-clipped).

The teacher starts the process by showing the first sentence on a screen or board, using the same opening procedure described earlier for arranging sentences. Then the teacher directs the students to arrange the rest of the sentences (on cards or strips, one for each student, or one for each pair of students) into a paragraph. There are paragraph read-alouds and discussions about plausibility. The students write their paragraph from their arrangement of sentences. There are two results. One, most every student writes a paragraph about James K. Polk. Two, everyone in the room knows more about James K. Polk than almost anyone, anywhere.

Every time students arrange and cluster sentences, they have another experience with paragraph thinking and writing. It is only a matter of how many times they do it before they *get* what paragraph thinking and writing mean. Then we provide more guidance.

Paragraph Completion (Fearn and Farnan 2001, 143–47): Grades 2–4, and Thereafter as Needed

Go back to the third grade. To establish prior knowledge, the teacher has read aloud from a biography of William Edward Burghardt Du Bois. (W. E. B. Du Bois, pronounced du-bois, not du-bwaa; he was American, not French. He pronounced his slave name as an American, not as his family's French owner might pronounce it.) The third grade read-aloud clarifies where he was born, what he achieved, and when he passed away. The teacher displays a paragraph frame on the board, document camera, or overhead screen.

> W. E. B. Du Bois was born in Massachusetts nearly 150 years ago. He went to college at. . . . He also went to. . . . During his life he. . . . He wrote. . . . At the age of 95. . . .

The teacher reads the opening sentence aloud. Several students also read it aloud. The teacher explains that while the first sentence is finished, the rest of the sentences are only started.

"So how do we think we should write the second sentence? Rachel?"
"He went to college at Tennessee and Harvard."
"Ronald?"
"And the college in Germany, too."
"Read the sentence, Ronald."
"He went to college in Tennessee, Harvard, and Germany."
"How about the third sentence? Alfonso?"
"I think the Germany college goes there."
"Read the sentence, then, Alfonso."
"He also went to college in Germany."
"Missy?"
"During his life he started the National Associ . . . shun. . . . I don't remember."
"Marcus?"
"The National Association for Colored People."
"The National Association for the Advancement of Colored People. You might have heard of the NAACP. That is what Du Bois started."
"Marcus?
"He wrote a book about black people's souls."
"*The Souls of Black Folk*, Marcus. Some day that would be a good book for everyone to read. Vanessa?"

"The last sentence is, 'He died in Africa when he was ninety-five.'"

"Boys and girls, look at the board to see what we have been talking about [the paragraph frame is on the board]. Everyone write the paragraph by writing the sentences. You have nine minutes before recess. I want your paragraphs on your way out the door."

That is a transcript from a recording of a partial third grade session with Paragraph Completion. There were twenty-nine third graders in the room. One student didn't write anything. Two students wrote the first and second sentences. Four students gave it a good try but didn't finish. Twenty-two students completed the paragraph, and every one read like a paragraph.

After recess, there was a short biographical review. During the last ten minutes of the literacy period the following morning, the teacher distributed sets of nine paragraph sentence cards (described earlier) about W. E. B. Du Bois for the students to sequence and break into main ideas. There was time for three students to read aloud from their arrangement. Every one was different, and every one was a plausible paragraph.

In two third grade lessons totaling thirty minutes, twenty-nine third graders learned enough of W. E. B. Du Bois to write a two-paragraph, and in one case a three-paragraph, biographical piece. The teacher followed those two sessions with two similar sessions about Ida B. Wells and Sojourner Truth.

WRITING EXTENDED DISCOURSE

Any writing after the first sentence is extended discourse, but for our purposes here, we are referring to whole pieces of writing of a paragraph or more. In the vernacular of English teachers, these are modes of discourse, short cues (Fearn and Farnan 2001, 166–72), and genres.

Read, Write, Share

To make social studies text more accessible, we need to include all of the students in the reading and writing. This is how to make that happen.

The students are assigned *The Rise of Islam* (Burstein and Shek 2006, 54–58), fifteen paragraphs over three pages of mostly four-color images and not-bad text. We directed seventh graders to read the material—"As much as you can as well as you can. You have one minute."

Several protested. "Now you have 58 seconds." Of the several, a few refused to participate. We ignored the behavior and quietly assured each of them that they need not participate if they chose not to, but they may not disturb anyone else. At the end of the minute, we called for everyone to stop reading, close the book (with a book mark in place) and write as much as they can as well as they can about what they read. "You have ninety seconds, one minute and a half." Most started to write. Those who had not read sat uninvolved. At ninety seconds, we said, "Finish the sentence you are writing right now, and stop." Many had stopped well before.

We asked for a reader and said if no one volunteers, we will call on someone. We called on a student we knew had something to read, because we were walking around the room during the ninety seconds and knew who had material that would move the activity forward. We directed everyone to listen to the reader and make a note of anything she read that is not on their papers. We had her read again and again—three times. Then another student three times and two more three times.

The reason for directing students to read three times is that most students haven't started to listen during the first read. During the second read, other students are adjusting their hearing to the sound of the reader's voice. During the third read, most students are listening and taking notes.

Most of the readers wrote much the same material. We directed the students to revise what they wrote by including whatever they heard from the readers. Most did. One of the nonparticipants did, too, because she had heard enough from listening to scribble a sentence.

Then we directed them back to the book to "read again as much as you can as well as you can in one minute." We gave them just over ninety seconds because most everyone was reading or writing. Then we repeated the protocol, again a third time.

"Close your book and cover your writing. We want to hear what you know about Muhammad, the beginnings of Islam, and the prophet's teaching." We called on several people we knew had enough to merit sharing aloud. Most shared similar information.

Then we directed them to read the next eight paragraphs and said that when they heard our little bell, they were to stop reading and write a sentence about whatever they were reading when they heard the bell. We sounded the bell three times during four minutes of reading.

The whole session took thirty-four minutes. The students deliberately attended to the material in the text. Of the four students who refused to participate, one wrote after the first "round," and one more wrote after the second round. Everyone else read the material and wrote about it, and every student in the room knew something about Muhammad and Islam when the thirty-four minutes had passed.

No teacher can make social studies text more interesting than it is, but we can focus students' attention. Read, Write, Share increases the probability that more students engage and, therefore, come to know what is in the chapter. They also write one or more paragraphs.

Summarizing

Summarizing means capturing the essence of a piece and minimally texturing it with relevant details. It is not "shorter and in your own words." We summarize in the social studies just as we thought in and wrote paragraphs.

Select a paragraph or two, or a page, from the social studies book, a biography, a description of the terrain on an Iowa farm, or, perhaps, a newspaper article.

Direct third, fourth, or fifth graders to make a t-chart that fills a whole sheet of 8.5" × 11" lined paper. They write main idea on the left of the t-chart and details on the right side of the t-chart.

Display on the screen or board the first line, not the first sentence, of the paragraph. "Read the line, think what it is about, and write a word or phrase on the left side of your t-chart to remind yourself what you think the line of text is about.

"On the right side of the t-chart write any little ideas you see in the line of text, any details, little ideas. Write details on the right side of your t-chart." Pause, but not long, and drop the mask down another line so two lines are displayed. They write a new main idea and add details.

Display the third line, and they write a new main idea and new details. Continue through the piece, one line at a time, until it is all displayed on the screen. Some students have a lot of main ideas and details, some only a few.

"Write a sentence that contains the best main idea you wrote on the left side of your t-chart. You have one minute."

"Look at your list of details or small ideas and put a '1' beside the detail that you think best explains your main idea sentence. Put a '2' beside the detail that you think is next best and a '3' beside the one you think is the next best. Write two sentences that include the three details.

"Now, write the last sentence for your one-paragraph summary."

Many of the fourth graders will have a passable summary. Remember, this is their first try. Tomorrow is another day, and if they do ten, most everyone will be writing pretty good summaries because while practice does not make perfect, informed practice makes better every time.

Sometimes, the district, the state, the school, or even the grade level team requires that one sentence gives bibliographical information. So write the bibliographic sentence and follow it with the previous four sentences. Maybe the summary has to have six or eight sentences. The point is that there are four essential sentences for the fourth graders' summary. No matter what a required summary includes, the essence of the summary is contained in the four sentences.

Describing

Describing is about making ideas and images live. Description exists in readers' minds, not writers' pages, as Stephen King, writer of extraordinary descriptions, tells us (King 2000, 173–180). The grain lives because of the image of waves. Words tell it is waist-high, and it moves with the breeze, but the image comes from waves in readers' minds.

The temperate rainforest on Washington's Olympic Peninsula is wet. Along the edges of Lake Quinault they measure rain in feet, not inches. Pure clear rainwater on the forest floor covers walkers' shoes with every step. Droplets on eyelashes from endless mist are temperate rainforest wet. It is also a description in locational geography.

All descriptions in the social studies should be within a few sentences, rarely more than one paragraph, and rarely more than eighty to one hundred words. There are reasons for the brevity.

One, there is almost nothing in elementary and middle school social studies that cannot be described within eighty to one hundred words, partly because that is about what fifth graders know.

Two, teachers are more likely to assign writing if the reading load is not overwhelming. Middle school teachers can have between 120 and 160 students per day. The two-page reading load from 120 to 160 students is overwhelming. If students write what they know rather than what teachers assign, the reading load is cut by three-quarters.

Three, people who make a living as writers routinely say that it is harder to write short than long. Precision and brevity are the watchwords in writing well (Fearn 1983).

Descriptive writing depends on nine attributes that help readers paint images and construct ideas.

Size: A small man could ride the motorcycle on his belt buckle.

Motion: He pushed the office recliner back slowly so every creak announced itself.

Position: Stopping just short of tipping over.

Shape: His belly bore testimony to years of trying to drink Canada Dry.

Color: He pinched the brown skin on her arm. "Skin color doesn't matter?"

Texture: The only person in the room whose hair was the enemy of a comb.

Atmosphere: The heat leaned on her, exhausted her by midmorning.

Mood: Silence enveloped the room when she walked in.

Order/disorder: Every machine parked in its place, every tool arranged by function, every bolt in its designated barrel, every child seated in the same chair in the same location.

When we teach students to describe, we teach them to think of and use one or more of the nine attributes of descriptive writing. "Describing words" tell; the attributes show.

Comparing and Contrasting

Perhaps the most powerful writing in the social studies is the one in which students rub two or more ideas against one other to show, for example, how the Declaration of Independence and the U.S. Constitution are both similar and different. Students have to know both documents.

Pennsylvania and Alabama are purported to be geographic sister states. How are Alabama and Pennsylvania geographically similar? How are they geographically different? How are Navajo and Chippewa similar and different?

The first paragraph in this section refers to similarities of and differences between the Declaration of Independence and the U.S. Constitution. A caller to a radio-talker said, "We have to remember the people who signed the Constitution." The Declaration of Independence and the Constitution are alike in that they are both founding documents; they are different in that the Founders signed the former.

The more a writer knows, the more complex compare and contrast writing becomes. The writing, itself, is not appreciably more complex than any other writing. It is thinking in similarities and contrasts that is so complex.

Start with a simple compare and contrast problem, at least on the surface, and age-appropriate for second graders.

"How are apples and bananas alike? Anna?"
"They're both fruit."
"Yes, Walter?"
"They both taste good."
"To you?"
"Yes. I love bananas."
"What if I don't love bananas? Are they still alike because they taste good?"

That is the hard part of compare and contrast writing. What we compare and contrast are alike and different because of what and how they are, not because of what and how we think they are, unless the writing is about the writer, not the fruit. If it is about the writer, the writer has to say so.

If we have that sort of conversation six times between January and May in the second grade, next year's teacher can ask how trains and airplanes are alike and different for transportation. Third graders can write how two biographical subjects are alike and different, how two stories in their literature book are alike and different, and how two photographs of the main street in their neighborhood look alike and different.

It is true that there is a substantial leap from apples and oranges to Abraham Lincoln and Jefferson Davis, but the principles are similar. Both examples (apples and bananas, Lincoln and Davis) demand sufficient knowledge of the subjects to show how they are similar and different. Both also require the ability to think and write in sentences that tell about similarities and differences. And both require regular practice comparing and contrasting properly.

Response to Reading

We ask our students to write about their reading. Usually what we want them to write is what they understood from their reading, and if response to reading is a high-stakes testing possibility, we want students to practice the state's protocol or formula.

For our purposes in the social studies, let us assume that writing in response to reading means a reader's response or reaction to the reading, which would mean we want each reader's response rather than a generic response that requires everyone to write the same way. The term for what we want in the social studies is "reader response." It comes from the seminal work of Louise Rosenblatt (1978) and research on implementation by Nancy Farnan (1989), the latter described next.

There are three reader response questions that ensure that thinking and writing are from the individual reader.

1. What did you notice from reading the chapter, biography, map, or other social studies material? If we ask that question, we are asking each reader what he noticed, and the noticing reflects the interaction between reader and text. The reader's prior knowledge influences what the reader notices. The first reader response question, therefore, honors the uniqueness of the individuals in the room.
2. What does the passage remind you of? When a student growing up on a small farm reads the first chapter of Gary Paulsen's *The Winter Room* (1989), he is reminded of many experiences very different from those of a student sitting alongside who has no sense of a manure pile or what "melty" means on a farm.
3. There is no formula for writing that reflects individual readers. If we want each reader's response, we have to ask for it. The two reader response questions ask for it.
4. How does it make you feel? Sometimes reading has affective content. When the Indian in *Stone Fox* (Gardiner 1980) stands just shy of the finish line, rifle at the ready, and says, "Anyone crosses the line, I shoot," the emotional loading is almost too much to bear.

Those are the three questions about readers' responses to reading. One or more can apply to any social studies reading. What do we want to know when we ask readers to write? We want to know if they got it. We want to know how they understand.

It is true that what students write to reader response directions may not follow a high-stakes testing formula for writing a response to reading. There are two ways to think about that.

One, consider that there might be a hundred thousand or more fifth graders writing to the high-stakes test, and scores of teachers trained to read and assign a rubric-based score. Think of the teacher-reader who, after reading and scoring several hundred formulaic papers, gets one that is personal, not formulaic, the one with a writer's voice that shows the connection between reader and text. How will the scorer rate that one?

Two, assign reader response questions for social studies writing, and the high-stakes test formula for literacy writing. When fifth graders ask why they are different, explain that there is more than one way to write in response to reading.

Essays That Share Opinions and Persuade Readers

Most of this book, and most of the social studies, is about perspectives, selections, and reflections of who we are. This book is a reflection of its writers. There is an audience, and the audience is broad. We cannot write about the social studies as though there were one social studies, and everyone teaches that one.

Readers have just read an opinion paragraph, the previous one, about content diversity in the social studies. Do you agree with the opinion? It wasn't written to make readers agree. We wrote it to share it. Readers have to decide to agree or disagree.

There are two kinds of writing in this section about opinion and persuasion. *Opinion* writing, like the opening paragraph, shares with an audience, "This is what I think."

The other kind of writing in this section is called *persuasion*. Persuasive writing shares with an audience, "This is what I think, and this is why you should think what I think." Writing to persuade presupposes that there are reasons why readers should think the way the writer thinks. A piece of writing persuades because there is merit in the argument, not because it has two reasons, or three or four. Good arguments persuade because they are informed and clear. If we have to write an assigned number of reasons, we probably don't have a good argument.

People who think an essay has to have a certain "look" need to read some George Will, who has been writing persuasive essays at least once each week for several decades. The only attribute of his essays that is consistent or predictable is its 750 words.

We used the word *essay* several times in the previous paragraphs. The word, and the form or genre, was invented in the sixteenth century by Michel de Montaigne, a French writer, who wrote to test his ideas about various subjects or topics (de Montaigne 1958; Boorstin 1998, 156). He wrote more than one hundred of what he called "trials," or explorations. The Latin word for his "trials" is *essai*, which has become Anglicized to *essay*. If he arrived at a conclusion, or what we refer to today as a "thesis statement," obviously it came at the end of his exploration or trial.

If we were true to historical origins in our writing assignments in the social studies, we would explain the essay as a trial or topic-driven exploration and model, on the screen as students observe, such essay thinking and writing. Then we would say, "You try it. Think of a biographical icon, a geographic form, a term in personal finance, a historical problem, and write a sentence, any sentence, associated with the topic you chose. You are writing to find out what you think about what you know."

Most students write something, and maybe half of those eventually think and write their way to a response to the question, "What do you think about your topic," or "Have you started to find your way to something like a conclusion?"

But this is school, and we do not have time to merely sit around and explore topics. If your school or district has a formula for what is called essay writing, teach it during literacy time so students can demonstrate it on demand. In social studies, write topical explorations.

Reports of Information

A fair number of reports of information, beginning in about the fourth grade, are at least partly to prepare students for next year's demand for reports of information. And fifth grade reports of information are at least partly in preparation for the sixth grade, and so forth until reports of information are in preparation for college.

Some sixth graders in an upper Midwest school district had an especially interesting middle school social studies teacher. Her academic major was anthropology, and in that major she took two courses in paleoanthropology, the study of the origins of homo sapiens from the fossil record.

She shared some of what she knew in the field, she shared parts of two audio lectures by eminent paleoanthropologists (Hawks 2011; King 2002), and she shared images of the fossil record, mostly skull and skull fragments and arm and leg bones. The students also toured the Neander Valley Museum near Dusseldorf in Germany via the museum's website (www.neanderthal.de/en/museum-valley/in-the-valley/index.html). Finally, the teacher shared some results of the research that mapped the human genome, particularly today's ability to follow mitochondrial DNA back many tens of thousands of years into the emergence of what she called "bipedal hominids."

Before she started the two-week unit, she featured a pizza and ice cream social in her classroom for parents. She called it "A Sixth Grade Journey into Human Origins" and invited parents and anyone else interested in discussing the unit. She made clear when she began that her pizza and ice cream social was not about permission. "This is what your sons and daughters will be learning in this two-week unit." Then she posted the state standard to which she was directing the unit: "Write an informative/explanatory essay that demonstrates knowledge gained about the science of human origins."

A parent stood and said, "Thank you for giving my daughter some real science." A man stood and turned to the rest of the parents. "I am the head pastor of the . . . church in. . . . I invite anyone to please call me with any concerns regarding this unit."

Three mothers asked in private if they could be in the classroom during the lessons. The teacher thanked them for their interest and asked them to make sure other parents knew that her classroom is always open to them. One student's mother and father emailed the teacher and said they would ask their daughter every night what she learned that day in social studies. The teacher replied, thanked them, and urged them to question their daughter thoroughly, every day throughout the year and come to the teacher with their questions.

We gave the teacher's plans five paragraphs because what the teacher did is part of the social studies. Throughout the two-week experience, the students wrote short KWL responses (This is what I learned, this is what I know, this is what I want to know more about) for six minutes every day. They wrote in composition books. Many students pestered her to know if she read what they wrote.

When the eight sessions were finished, the teacher asked the students to make a list of what they learned from the unit that was especially interesting. They could use their composition books to remind them of what they learned. She said they had to list at least two ideas, but not more than five.

When they finished their lists, the teacher revealed the writing task on the document camera.

"Put a '1' beside the item you think is the most interesting to you, a '2' beside the idea you think is the next most interesting, then a '3,' a '4,' and a '5' if you have that many. Write at least one sentence but not more than three sentences to explain each of your items. Then rewrite each of your items and the explanatory sentences on a separate sheet of paper. Leave four blank lines at the top of your page. You have fifteen minutes."

At fifteen minutes, the teacher told the students they had to write one or two sentences to introduce their report and one or two sentences to end their report, and those would be two separate paragraphs. After another ten minutes, most of the students had a report of information that was as long as seven paragraphs and as brief as four paragraphs. Every report had an introduction, a close, and two to five paragraphs in-between. The students' reports were copied so one stayed in the room and one went home.

Every reader of this page has written many reports of information in a traditional manner, so every reader knows how to teach those reports. We have suggested two alternative possibilities. Readers have to decide.

SENTENCES AND WORD STUDY

There are two additional areas of content that constitute the foundations for writing well. One is thinking and writing in sentences. The other is word study for writing (vocabulary and spelling). This chapter, however, is about writing in the social studies. We have focused on what students write during social studies time. It is not about teaching writing during literacy time.

There are several points relevant to thinking and writing in sentences and to word study for writing that must be addressed in writing instruction during literacy time.

1. Teaching sentence thinking and writing properly is not about subjects and predicates, "complete" thoughts, capital letters, and periods. We have hoards of students who know those and still write sentences at least tentatively, if not badly.
2. Second graders can learn to write compound sentences very well, and third graders can learn to write complex sentences. By the end of the fourth grade, it is reasonable to expect that nearly all students can think in and write the variety of literate sentences.
3. The sequence for teaching sentence thinking and writing begins with simple sentences, then relationships between and among sentences, compound sentences, complex sentences, and combinations of sentences to make ideas and images.
4. The reason why so few students write with the words we teach for vocabulary development is because we teach vocabulary for recognition (reading), while writers need recall vocabulary. The two are very different. Put another way, readers need meanings for words; writers need words for meanings.
5. With respect to spelling, the first sound we hear when we read "mat" is (mmm). The first sound we hear when we spell the word "mat" is the name of the first letter. We read with sounds. We spell with the names of letters and clusters of letters. Spelling is about letters and letter clusters. "Sound it out" might be a reasonable clue for reading, but never for spelling.
6. The only reason for a spelling test is to ensure that everyone in the room learns that she is an effective speller, every time. If we teach spelling as the sounds of letter names and clusters, in segments so there are never more than four- to five-letter and cluster sounds to remember, and we ensure that every student is attending deliberately to how each word is spelled, every student will earn at least 80 percent, every time.

We began this chapter by asserting that we (the profession) have to rethink *what* we teach when we teach students to write. We gave a cursory explanation of what that means in the genres and modes of discourse likely to appear in social studies writing. A more complete presentation of writing in the social studies would be a book of more than two hundred pages. This is a chapter in a less than two-hundred-page book. We finish as we began. We selected what to include from among many worthy possibilities.

REFERENCES

Boorstin, Daniel J. 1998. *The Seekers: The Story of Man's Continuing Quest to Understand His World.* New York: Random House.

Borneman, Walter R. 2008. *Polk: The Man Who Transformed the Presidency and America.* New York: Random House.

Burstein, Stanley M., and Richard Shek. 2006. *World History: Medieval to Early Modern Times.* New York: Holt, Rinehart and Winston.

De Montaigne, Michel. 1958. *Essays.* London: Penguin.

Farnan, Nancy. 1989. "Reading and Responding: Effects of a Prompted Approach to Literature." *The California Reader* 22 (4): 5–8.

Fearn, Leif. 1983. "The Art of Brevity." *Writers West* 1 (7): 3–5.

Fearn, Leif, and Nancy Farnan 2001. *Interactions: Teaching Writing and the Language Arts.* Boston: Houghton Mifflin.

———. 2007. "The Influence of Professional Development on Young Writers' Writing Performance." *Action in Teacher Education* 29 (2): 17–28.

———. 2007. "When Is a Verb: Using Functional Grammar to Teach Writing." *Journal of Basic Writing* 26 (1): 63–87.

Gardiner, John Reynolds. 1980. *Stone Fox.* New York: Harper and Row.

Hawks, John. 2011. "The Rise of Humans: Great Scientific Debates." Audio Lecture. Chantilly, VA: The Teaching Company.

King, Barbara J. 2002. "Biological Anthropology: An Evolutionary Perspective." Audio Lecture. Chantilly, VA: The Teaching Company.

King, Stephen. 2000. *On Writing.* New York: Scribner.

Paulsen, Gary. 1989. *The Winter Room.* New York: Scholastic.

Pearson, P. David, and Gallagher, Margaret C. 1983. *The Instruction of Reading Comprehension.* Technical Report 297, Center for the Study of Reading, Champaign: University of Illinois at Urbana-Champaign.

Rosenblatt, Louise M. 1978. *The Reader, The Tex, The Poem: The Transactional Theory of the Literary Work.* Carbondale: Southern Illinois University Press.

About the Authors

Leif Fearn completed teacher preparation at Shippensburg State College, now Shippensburg University, and two graduate degrees at Arizona State University. He has taught students through the elementary and middle school grades. He served the Navajo tribe in its initial experiment in tribal education that led to their K–12, community college, and cooperative university at Rough Rock, Arizona. He later served in Indian Community Action with responsibilities for educational training among fifty-five southwestern tribes. On the faculty at San Diego State University, he served primarily in teacher education and special education; in the former in literacy and social studies and the latter working with teachers of gifted and talented and mildly disabled students. His work in writing instruction, gifted and talented education, and creative thinking and problem solving has appeared widely in publication over the years. He and Nancy have five children and eight grandchildren.

Eric Fearn completed his undergraduate studies in Spanish and history at San Diego State University. He taught middle school English immersion at Monterrey Tech in Chihuahua, Mexico; elementary and middle school Spanish immersion in San Diego, California; and elementary and middle school Spanish immersion in Lakeside, California. He was recognized as his district's Teacher of the Year for his classroom excellence and his leadership in language immersion programs. Eric is husband to Grace and father to Colleen, Emilio, and Qui Que.